London Tales

WORD OF MOUTH
Antoinette Moses

UNDERGROUND
Sue Leather

TRAVELLING LIGHT
Jane Spiro

© 2003 - **ELI** s.r.l.
P.O. Box 6 - Recanati - Italy
Tel. +39/071/75 07 01 - Fax +39/071/97 78 51
E-mail: info@elionline.com - www.elionline.com

Editor
Maria Cleary

Series editors
Antoinette Moses
Alan Pulverness

Illustrations
Andrea Goroni

Printed in Italy - Tecnostampa - Recanati   03.83.190.0

ISBN 88-536-0041-1

CONTENTS

Preface

This volume of new English fiction contains three stories, all of which are set in London.

The first story, *Word of Mouth,* takes the reader into contemporary London, the London portrayed by glossy magazines, the world of models and advertising. It examines the reality beneath the images and poses some challenging questions about how we accept what is projected by advertisers.

The second story, *Underground,* shows how, in a large city like London, people's lives are invariably linked to a network of other people they don't necessarily know. The Underground train system acts as a metaphor for this network of visible and invisible connections.

In the third story, *Travelling Light,* a Londoner comes back to the city he had left many years ago. This is a story in which London is seen through the eyes of a stranger, a man who has lost touch with the city of his birth. It shows how cities can change yet stay the same.

ANTOINETTE MOSES

Word of
Mouth

About the Author

Antoinette Moses has, among numerous other occupations, written all her life. She has been a journalist, an editor, a film festival director and a cook. She has published a guide to Athens, a guide to running arts festivals, a cookery book and a book of poetry, as well as six original EFL readers. She has also co-written the scripts for two EFL videos and has written a novel, a novel for children and four plays, one for BBC Radio 4. She has also written and presented two television series for Channel 4.

Ask the Author

Where did the idea for this story come from?

From two newspaper articles. One was about people selling drinks and cigarettes in the way that is described in this story, by word of mouth. The other was about using 'alpha pups', children who are seen to be popular and fashionable, and giving them new computer games to play with in the playground so that other kids want the same games. I was quite disturbed by these stories, particularly the latter, where children are being manipulated by large corporations. Then I started to think about how people are manipulated by advertising and the media.

The background for the story came from reading lifestyle articles in Sunday magazines. From these I found out about the redeveloped Docklands flats and what they look like and the kind of people who live in them. The articles also provided me with a view of a world where fashion is all-important. I watched television documentaries about models and listened to what they said about their lives. I felt that they lived in a very different world from the one I – and indeed most people – live in, and I wanted to show that in the story.

Do you get most of your ideas from newspaper articles?

No. Ideas come from all kinds of sources. They come from books as well as newspapers, from history, from photographs and from stories people tell. What often happens is that I read something in a newspaper, or hear something on the radio or on television, and it sows an idea in my brain. Then a few days later, I may hear a conversation or read something else which connects with the first idea. Once I've got an idea, I start to research it and then later begin to add the characters who will bring the story to life.

However, that is not the only way my stories begin. Sometimes I begin with characters. These may be characters I know or have met – often I put bits of different people in a character – or they may be people I see across a room or on a train. I observe people a lot and I have to confess that I love listening to other people's conversations. I never go anywhere without a notebook, and if I see anything unusual or hear a great remark, I note it down. These notes can be very short.

What do you try to achieve in a short story?

That's a difficult question. Mostly, I just want to tell a story that people want to read. But I also use stories to express how I feel about the world. I feel that being a writer is a responsibility and if we hold a mirror up to the world, then we have a duty to make what is reflected in that mirror as truthful as possible. I have strong views on what I feel is just and good and what is unjust and bad, and I worry about many world issues. I always feel that if I can make even one or two people think about an issue, then my work is not without some worth. But I don't want to preach. I'm a storyteller, not a politician, and I want people to enjoy my stories. But I like to make people think, too. In this story, I hope readers will wonder whether it is possible for a political party to manipulate people in this way, and start to think about how

7

they are influenced in their consumer choices.

All my stories are different, but in all of them I try to create believable characters and settings. I always do a lot more research than I end up using!

Do you imagine a particular kind of reader when you're writing?

No, not really. I tend to write the kind of stories that I'd like to read. I certainly don't write stories thinking that they are for people learning English. If I have an imaginary reader looking over my shoulder as I write, it's usually a friend, and I can visualise them reading the story and liking some of it. Since I often use my own experiences, I imagine people who know me well reading those sections and laughing. But generally, no, I don't think of the reader as I write; the story just takes off and I follow as well as I can.

Before Reading

The phrase 'word of mouth' means speaking to people. It is used in this story to describe the process of selling things by getting fashionable people to talk about them and say how good they are.

(A)   Now you know what 'word of mouth' means, what kind of story do you think this will be?

        tragic   ☐

        humorous   ☐

        old-fashioned ☐

        contemporary ☐

        frightening   ☐

(B)   Have you ever bought or done anything because all your friends were talking about it? Give examples.

....
....
....
....

(C)   Read the first line of the story. What kind of person do you think is talking? Who do you think is being addressed?
Give reasons for your choice.

....
....
....
....

Word of Mouth

Hi! How are you? Great to see you! Hi there!

You smile, you don't know me, but you want to. I can see that. I'm the guy* ... I'm the action* ... what's cool* ... where it's at*. I'm what you dream about when you think of city life. I'm so cool you could use me as an ice pack*.

I come into your bar. You look at me. Of course you do. You couldn't miss me. It's my designer look*, the jeans, the jacket I'm holding by one finger over my shoulder. It's the shades*, pushed up onto my head. You want to know where I shop, you want to know who I am.

10   "Hi!" I call to the girl behind the bar. She smiles at me. Girls all smile at me. I smile back. I have an amazing smile.

"I'll have a Driver's Special," I say. She smiles and brings me my drink. It looks cool. I take it and wander* over to a table. Slowly. You are all watching me. I smile round the room at you all. Then I turn and look at the door. A beautiful girl is coming into the bar. She looks like a model. Of course she does. She is a model. She's with another cool guy. Of course she is. Perhaps they are in love. They look very happy.

"Hey, Julie!" I call. The beautiful girl waves at me.

"Hi, Ben!" But she doesn't come over to speak to me. She is talking to
20   the guy with her. They laugh. You are all watching them now.

---

the guy: (here) the ideal/perfect man
the action: everything fashionable that is going on
cool: (used as word of approval) fashionable; good.
where it's at: what is fashionable
ice pack: container of frozen gel used
for sports injuries/to reduce inflammation
designer look: image created by wearing clothes by well-known designers
shades: sunglasses
wander over: walk slowly and casually towards a place or person

Julie and her friend come over to the bar. They smile at the girl behind the bar.

"What would you like to drink?" asks the bar girl.

"Oh, I'll have a Driver's Special," says Julie. "What about you, Pete?" she asks her friend.

"The same for me," says Pete.

Pete and Julie take their drinks across to a table. They talk to each other and laugh. They look like a couple in a movie*. You're watching them. You're thinking: yes, that is how you look when you are in love. You're thinking: I'd like to look like that. You're thinking: I'd like to have a girlfriend or a boyfriend who looks like that.

Quite soon some of you will order a Driver's Special. Of course you will. It's cool, isn't it? It's because we're cool and we're drinking it.

After a few minutes I get ready to leave the bar. "Hey, Ben!" calls Julie. "Where are you off to?"

"*Tin Pan Alley*," I call out. "Where else *is* there?"

"See you later," calls Julie.

And so she does, but not in *Tin Pan Alley*. No. We're in another bar, where we act out the same scene. It's what we do. Of course if you watch us closely, you'll see that we don't actually drink our Driver's Specials. It's disgusting, a kind of non-alcoholic cocktail. We're paid to

movie: film

order it, we don't have to drink it.

We're paid? Of course we are. That's what we do. We are the latest marketing tools*, we are the cutting edge* of advertising. We advertise new products by word of mouth.

Does it work? Yes, of course it does. Because I and Julie and Pete, her friend in the bar, and a few others, are the people you want to be.

The idea isn't new. Go to a movie and what do you see? The hero, the Tom Cruise, the Jude Law, the latest star, picks up a can and drinks.
50 You can see the brand*. And you can see the kind of jeans he's wearing. You think it's accidental*? Of course it isn't. Someone paid to advertise that drink. Someone paid for him to wear those jeans. It's called product placement. Movies have being doing it for years.

And now there's us. We're the living movies. We're product placement, but we're not on the screen. We're in a club or bar near you.

In the States they use cool kids, too. They have a name for them: "alpha pups." They are paid to play the latest games. And it works. One new computer game became a hit* in a weekend after a few alpha pups were seen playing it. Word of mouth, you see.

60 So I'm what they call the alpha* male. You want to look like me? So you buy the designer jeans I wear and drink the drinks I pretend to drink and go to the clubs I pretend to go to. It's so simple.

marketing tools: methods used to sell an item, e.g. an advertisement, posters, television commercials
cutting edge: newest and most advanced
brand: name of a product made by a specific company
accidental: casual; not planned
hit: success
alpha male: zoological term for the leader of the pack

Naturally everything is worked out in advance. You can't just go into any bar. I mean if I went into a tough* East End pub looking like this and ordered a drink called Driver's Special, someone might just decide to punch* my face in. And it's a beautiful face, you have to admit that. I don't want anyone to punch it.

There is a back-up* team, of course, and the bar staff all know who we are. Well, they have to, don't they? Otherwise I can just imagine the scene. I walk into the bar and give my order and the bar girl turns round and says:

"Driver's Special? You must be joking. It's disgusting. If you're driving, why don't you have a coffee?"

And that would not be cool, would it?

And so here we are: Pete and Julie and me at the end of the evening. We're not at *Tin Pan Alley*. It's not the kind of club we like. We went to the opening* and you can see photographs of us there, but we don't go there for pleasure*. No, we're back at my Docklands* apartment, sitting on the balcony watching* the world below go by, looking at the slow ripples* on the River Thames. We're eating pizza from the local delivery place and listening to a Travis CD. We're having fun at last. We're ourselves.

---

tough East End pub: pub in the east of London where you might find tough (strong and/or dangerous) people
punch my face in: hit my face very hard
back-up team: group of people that will help if needed
opening: party to open a gallery or shop

pleasure: enjoyment; fun
Docklands: area of East London that was originally London's docks and now has fashionable offices and flats.
watching the world go by: watching people go past
ripples: very small waves on the surface of the water

You see the thing is we're much more like you than you think. We want to have fun with our mates*, too. We go to movies together and to clubs and bars. The only difference is the way we look. There was a phrase for it back in the Sixties – the Beautiful People. I think it was the Beatles who used it first.

Well, that's us. We're today's Beautiful People. But the world is different today. Today if you're beautiful, you're a commodity*, you're somebody
90 with something that everyone else wants. You're for sale.

Ben looks around his Docklands apartment – that's the word he always uses – he prefers the American term*. "Flat", he considers, is a rather flat little word, it does not have the expansive* sense of apartment, which sounds so much more international. An apartment could be anywhere, in New York or Paris, or here above the Thames, with one of the best views in the capital.

This, thinks Ben, is what he has always dreamed of, what he wanted even before he knew he wanted it. This world, this view, this life; it was so far from the semi-detached* house on the outskirts* of Ipswich
100 where he grew up. His father left home when he was twelve years old and his mother worked at the local chemist's. She always wanted him to study pharmacy, "a proper profession", she used to say, "and you don't have to wear a uniform."

mates: friends
commodity: something that can be sold
term: (here) word
expansive: spacious

semi-detached house: house joined to the one next door
outskirts: outer area of a city or town

His mother has always been suspicious* of uniforms. Ben's father had been a postman, and Ben sometimes wondered whether his mother's dislike of her former husband had spread to anything that she might associate with him. Ben tries not to think too much about the past. It makes him frown* and frowning creates wrinkles*. That's what Julie always says, but at nineteen her skin is still firm and supple*.

110 Ben pads* around his apartment, filling up glasses, changing the music, playing the host, enjoying the evening, enjoying his home. The apartment is a square box, large, lofty*, with red-brick walls and blue-painted wrought-iron* stairs. Like the other apartments in the vast former warehouse, it is open-plan*, with huge windows overlooking the river. Once tea and cotton were hauled* up onto these wooden floorboards. Today rich young men and women cover them with oriental rugs and Japanese-style futons*. The building contains a hundred individual apartments, a gym, an indoor swimming pool and a basement parking area.

120 Ben's mother no longer lives in a semi*; he has bought her a small cottage in a village just outside Ipswich. She continues to work, although she doesn't need to. Ben has bought her an annuity*, but she needs the company*, she tells him. "What would I do all day by myself? Watch the telly*? I'd go crazy."

suspicious: distrusting, when you have a bad feeling about someone or thing
frown: draw one's eyebrows together in an angry or worried expression
wrinkles: deep lines on the face
supple: soft and flexible
pads: walks quietly, like a cat
lofty: tall, with high ceilings
wrought-iron: iron twisted to make decorative balconies or staircases

open-plan: the main rooms open, with no internal walls
hauled up: pulled up
futons: low Japanese beds
semi: semi-detached house
annuity: sum of money invested to provide an annual income
company: contact with other people
telly: television

Ben brought his mother to see his new apartment last year, but the visit was not a great success.

"For that price you could have a nice new house with a double garage and a private swimming pool," she complained. "Why on earth do you want to live in a draughty* old place like this?"

130 "I like the history," Ben told her, though it had been Sally, his girlfriend, who had appreciated the history, not him. In the communal areas of the building are memorabilia of the old trading days: an anchor*, a bit of a barrel*, a piece of cotton sacking*. They are all framed with small cards giving their history, as if they were in a museum. And Ben supposes in a way they are.

"They used to store tea here in huge sacks," he told his mother. "You see that pulley* there, that's where they'd unload the ships. The ships used to come right up the Thames in those days. Now they just go to the big container* ports down river. This building is a museum to the 140 past. It's part of our heritage*," he added. He was trying to impress her, but was not quite sure why.

"The place must have been alive* with rats," commented his mother. "Goodness knows what it smelled like." She sniffed* around her as if the smell of decaying* tea or dead rodents* might still be present. In a neighbouring warehouse apartment that once housed coffee, the faint

draughty: not well insulated, so that you can feel the cold blowing through
anchor: large hook-shaped piece of metal dropped by boats to stop them moving
barrel: round wood container used for storage
sacking: material used to make sacks
pulley: wheel over which a rope is hung used to bring up goods
container ports: ports where boats load and unload goods in large metal containers onto and from lorries
heritage: history and tradition
alive with rats: full of rats
sniffed: breathed in loudly through her nose, a sound of disapproval
decaying: the process of being destroyed through natural causes
rodents: rats and mice

scent of coffee beans remains like an olfactory* ghost. Ben did not tell his mother this.

So here he is on a warm summer evening; sitting on the balcony looking over the river. The tourist boats have been tied up for the night and only the occasional barge* chugs* up the river. Below Ben's apartment there's the usual background buzz* of voices and laughter from the café bar next door, the sound of rich young people having fun.

"Is it true that Madonna came here last week?" asks Julie.

"No. It's just a story," says Ben, stretching his feet up against the balcony. "I think the girl who lives upstairs used to know Guy Ritchie, though."

"So Mrs* Ritchie might have popped* in?" continues Julie, who is a big fan of Madonna.

"Sure," murmurs Ben. "Why not?"

"Cool," says Julie.

If Ben were to categorise this conversation, he would say it was typical. He might even say that it summed* up his life. There was Julie establishing that she was in a place where Madonna might drop* in.

---

olfactory: to do with the sense of smell
barge: flat-bottomed boat used to carry goods on rivers and canals
chugs: moves slowly and noisily
buzz: low sound; also the sound of bees

Mrs Ritchie: Guy Ritchie's wife, (here: the singer, Madonna)
popped in: visited
summed up: described in a few words
drop in: visit

The facts – had Madonna visited the apartment above? – were not important. What mattered was that this was a building where Madonna might drop in. The image was right for Julie. She was sitting in a place not so far from where Madonna might sit. It was the same as Ben creating an image for thousands of others to copy. They might not see him, but if they drank the same drinks or smoked the same brands, they
170   might look a bit like him. If they visited the right clubs, they might even see him.

Julie is sitting like a ballet dancer with one long leg hanging sideways over the arm of her chair. She has long dark hair that looks as if someone has polished it or as if she's been groomed* like a prize racehorse. Young and glossy*, she is exactly what the magazines want. She and her friends are not just models, they also feature* in magazine editorials. They are the new celebrities*: the cooks, the actors, the fashion designers, the successes, the new A-list* in town, the people at the most glamorous openings. And they open so many things:
180   restaurants, clubs, shops, galleries and even movies.

Julie cannot count how many openings she has been to; Ben would not want to. He is bored, but does not admit it, even to himself. But he enjoys Julie's company, her mindless* chatter. She's an old friend, but not his girlfriend. Sally is Ben's girlfriend, but Sally is in New York for the summer. Ben is pretending that this is a temporary separation, that Sally got a work offer she couldn't refuse. He is not thinking about the row* he and Sally had before she left. Or the row before that. Ben can't remember what it was about; there have been so many rows. He tries to

---

groomed: cleaned and polished (like a horse)
glossy: shiny; polished
feature: are written about
celebrities: famous people

A-list: the most famous people; those most wanted at parties and openings
mindless chatter: meaningless conversation
row: argument

forget them. He emails silly jokes to Sally every night and tells no-one
190   that she never answers.

To think about the arguments, the rows, the fights, would mean
examining his life and Ben does not want to do that. He enjoys his life.
He enjoys his lifestyle*. He does not want to think how his advertising
cigarettes could affect kids.

"I don't tell them to start smoking," he had argued when Sally had told
him to turn* down the job.

"No, but kids copy you. You know that. They want to look like you.
They want to be like you."

"You enjoy the money, don't you?" he'd replied. He had not liked her
200   reply. He wanted to think that she needed him, that the apartment
meant the same to her as it did to him. He didn't like to think that he
had changed. Sometimes, he thought, Sally sounded just like his mother.

He watches the river and listens to Julie and Pete talk about a book
someone they know has read. Julie never sounds like Ben's mother. Pete
is half-French and is saving money to become a photographer. Ben has
never seen him holding a camera, only in front of one.

"Did you taste that stuff, that new drink?" asks Pete.

"Yes," says Julie. "I had the odd* sip. Isn't it disgusting? I wonder
what's in it?"

---

lifestyle: the way one lives; the activities one enjoys

turn down: refuse; say no to
odd sip: small drink from time to time

210   "Chemicals, I imagine" says Ben. "Lots of synthetic* flavourings. What do you think it's meant to taste like?"

None of them is sure. They think it might be cherry, or coffee, or blackcurrant. It doesn't matter. They know it's going to be a huge success.

"See you for lunch at the *Paradise Bar*?" asks Ben as the evening comes to an end. This is less a question, more a form of farewell*.

"No, I'm not going there any more," Julie replies.

"Why not?" They are amazed. They always go there. It's where they have lunch.

220   "Because they were incredibly rude the last time I went," Julie explains. She tells them the story. It's a story that they know could have happened to them, though they don't say this.

"You know my mother was coming up from the country last week," begins Julie. "Well, I wanted to take her round London, take her shopping, give her some treats. Mum lives in a village near Taunton*, she works for a small company that makes conservatories*, she does the books* and things. But she doesn't often come* up to London and she doesn't know any of the places we go to."

---

synthetic flavourings: chemicals used to create flavours
farewell: goodbye
Taunton: town in south-west England
conservatories: rooms, mostly of glass, added to houses as an extra room or to grow plants and flowers
does the books: adds up the figures; does the accounts
come up to: visit (one always goes 'up' to London)

Ben and Pete nod. None of their families know the places they go to.

230   "So," continues Julie. "I took her to *Dan's* for breakfast, and then we went shopping in Knightsbridge, and then I booked my usual table at the *Paradise* for lunch."

They nod again. This was a good schedule*, this was the kind of tour that one gave to mothers. It included all the places where they went every day and places where their parents might even bump* into someone off the telly, or from the movies. They know their parents enjoy celebrity-spotting*. It gives them something to talk about when they go back home.

"And then?" asks Pete, tipping* back his chair and pressing his feet
240   against the wrought-iron balcony.

"Then, when we get to the *Paradise* and they see Mum, they tell me my usual table is full and put us right at the back near the kitchen door."

"You're joking!" explodes Ben. Nobody wants to sit at the back of the room. Only tourists get the table by the kitchen door.

"It's true. And the service was awful and they made Mum feel so uncomfortable. I wanted Mum to have anything she wanted, so she ordered a pudding, it was apple tart with cream. I know that we'd never look at something like that, it must contain a whole day's calories, but Mum doesn't care. I mean it's not like Mum's fat, but she loves her food
250   – she's a great cook – and she's quite big. Well, she's Mum and I like her

---

schedule: timetable   celebrity-spotting: seeing celebrities
bump into: meet by accident   tipping back: making one's chair lean backwards

how she is. And anyway she was on holiday. So she ate it and enjoyed it. Then the waitress, it was Terri, you know how thin she is, she looked at Mum and said in a horrible voice: 'I can see you enjoyed your pudding,' and Mum went bright* red. It ruined her day."

"That's awful," commiserates* Pete. "You're right not to go back. I won't go there either."

"Nor me," says Pete. "They can't be allowed to behave like that."

"No," says Ben, thoughtfully. "We ought to do something ... something more than just boycott* the place ourselves." He pauses. He has an 260 idea.

"Listen," he says. "I think I've got a plan." His friends turn to him. They are listening.

"You know how when we say how good a place is, everyone goes there ..." he begins.

"Yeah," says Julie.

"Well, what if we did it the other way round? If we went around saying how awful a place was?"

"But isn't that slander*?" asks Pete.

"Only if we say something that's untrue. We don't actually say it's bad.

---

bright red: very red
commiserates: shows sympathy
boycott: avoid using a company or product

slander: spoken statement that damages someone's reputation

270 We just say that we don't go there any more. We say we don't like it. And that's true, we don't."

"Of course," says Pete. "Ben, you're a genius!"

And that's what they do. Over the next couple of weeks, everywhere they go, they call out: "Are you going to the *Paradise Bar*?" and one or other of them says: "Oh no, I don't go there any more. I've gone* off it completely."

They watch the effect their words have on others. They notice how soon other people, for no reason, are saying that they themselves no longer go to the *Paradise Bar*. After a couple of weeks, they don't even have to say 280 it any more. No-one in their crowd goes to the *Paradise*.

gone off it: don't like it

Word of Mouth

A month later Ben, Julie and Pete walk down Charles Street, past the *Paradise* to see what has happened. The restaurant is almost empty, only a couple of middle-aged tourists inside sit at front tables that a few weeks before they would never have been given. The *Paradise* looks like a restaurant about to give up the ghost*. The celebrity chef* has already given in his notice* and the owners are having emergency meetings with their accountants. Ben, Julie and Pete have achieved their goal. They have closed a restaurant.

290 In *Lola Runs!*, their new favourite café bar, they drink champagne to celebrate. But despite a bottle of vintage* Bollinger, Julie is unusually quiet.

"Aren't you pleased?" Ben asks her. "You've done it! You've closed the *Paradise*."

"Yes," she frowns. She is trying to put her thoughts into words and it is not so easy. "I know we should be happy, but don't you boys think it's scary*? I mean we've got the power to open things and close them. People do what they think we're doing."

"What's the problem?" Ben laughs and pours himself another drink. "Let's drink to power," he says, lifting his glass. "Here's to success.
300 Here's to power over the people!"

"That's a dangerous toast*," says a quiet voice behind him.

---

give up the ghost: die ('ghost' here = spirit, soul)
celebrity chef: famous cook, possibly one who appears on television
given in his notice: told his employers he is leaving

vintage Bollinger: expensive brand of champagne
scary: frightening
toast: lifting one's glass and drinking to honour or celebrate something

They turn round quickly, then see who it is and laugh. Lawrence is their agent*. Ben and Peter and Julie like him. He's good. He gets them good jobs and worries about details. A good agent, Ben often says, is a man who cares about details. Lawrence is such a man. He makes sure that the tickets have all been bought, that the hotels are good enough, that his models get timetables in advance. Lawrence's father was in the army and sometimes Lawrence thinks he must have inherited* his organisational* skills, though his father cannot* stand what Lawrence
310   does or how he looks and has not spoken to him for many years.

Lawrence is more than an agent to Ben and his fellow-models*, he is a friend. They can talk to Lawrence, and they do so now. They tell him all about the *Paradise Bar.*

"Really?" murmurs* Lawrence, and he goes very quiet. He's thinking about something, notes Ben. Lawrence, Ben has observed, always goes quiet when he's thinking.

"Well," says Lawrence, a few minutes later. "Maybe you can help me. This is a favour*. I don't want you to do it unless you want to." But he knows they will want to.

320   The favour is to repeat their *Paradise* trick. This time it's a designer. They don't ask what he has done, but they know there's a feud* of some sort. So they do what Lawrence asks; they stop wearing the designer's clothes and say how boring the label* has become. They say that no-one

---

agent: person who finds work for actors, models etc. and takes a percentage of their pay
inherited: acquired genetically
organisational skills: ability to organise
cannot stand: strongly dislikes; hates

fellow-models: the models who work with him
murmurs: whispers; speaks softly
favour: something done in order to please someone, because they are a friend
feud: long-standing argument
label: brand of clothes

wears his clothes any more. Soon everyone stops wearing his clothes. Then Lawrence and the designer have a meeting and the feud is settled. They start wearing the designer's clothes again and modelling them, too. Lawrence is delighted. He gives them a bonus*.

And so Ben's life goes on. He wears the latest clothes, drinks the newest drinks and visits the smartest bars. He opens places and, just
330   occasionally, for special friends, he closes them.

Then Lawrence introduces Ben and his friends to Mr Woodhouse.

They are sitting in *Lola Runs!,* drinking iced espressos and gossiping*, when Lawrence brings Mr Woodhouse to meet them. The models look at the newcomer* suspiciously. He doesn't look right, they think, he doesn't look like anyone they know. His suit is too tight and he's wearing the kind of blue striped tie that their fathers might have worn to the office. He doesn't look cool, they think. But they smile at him because he's with Lawrence, because he might be a client and because smiling is their natural* reflex.

340   Lawrence introduces Mr Woodhouse. It seems that he's an old school friend.

"We go back a long way*," says Lawrence. "I'd like you to do him and me a favour," he adds smiling, knowing that they will agree.

"It's usual rates of course. Not a freebie*," adds Lawrence which is odd because either it's business or it's a favour. But they say nothing, as

---

bonus: extra money
gossiping: talking about other people and their private lives
newcomer: new person
natural reflex: action that occurs naturally

which one cannot stop oneself doing
we go back a long way: we have known each other for a long time
freebie: free service or thing

Lawrence is their boss and they never say no to money.

"What's the product?" Ben remembers to ask. "Is it a restaurant?" Mr Woodhouse, he has decided, looks like the kind of man who buys a restaurant without knowing the business and then wonders why no-one comes. There are lots of restaurants like that. They usually last* around two months; sometimes they don't even last a few weeks.

Lawrence doesn't answer Ben's question, he just smiles and pats* his models on the back in a contented, avuncular* fashion. A day or two later, Ben realises why. There isn't any product. The product is Mr Woodhouse himself. For some reason, that Ben can't figure* out, Mr Woodhouse wants to be one of them, one of the A-list, or at least that is what he wants other people to think.

The models don't enjoy his company and grumble* about him amongst themselves. Mr Woodhouse isn't one of them and he doesn't fit* in, but they play* out the charade* and pretend that he's one of the gang. They go into bars and clubs and restaurants in their usual way and then Mr Woodhouse comes in. Mr Woodhouse waves and they wave back. Then he joins the group and they all sit round a table talking together.

Actually, Ben has observed, Mr Woodhouse doesn't talk much. He laughs a lot, a strange, tinny* laugh, and pretends that they are all having a great time together. But he doesn't actually laugh at anything anyone says. Ben has decided he doesn't like Mr Woodhouse.

last: (here) remain open
pats: touches with one's hand
avuncular: (literally) like an uncle; giving the impression that one is superior
figure out: understand

grumble: complain
fit in: be part of a group
play out: play to the end
charade: something that is not true
tinny: with a thin sound, like metal

"Who is he?" he asks Pete one afternoon. It has been bothering* him, this game, this pretend friendship.

370 "Does it matter?" Pete replies.

"Of course it matters."

"Why?" asks Pete. "We're being paid aren't we?" And he changes the subject and starts to talk about a new car he's read about and which he thinks he might buy to replace his Porsche.

Now Ben can't stop thinking about Mr Woodhouse. He wonders whether it's simply that he's become a snob*, that he doesn't like being seen with anyone who isn't cool, which is something else that Sally accused him of before she left for New York. But this time he thinks that this isn't the reason. It's the strangeness of it all. Why does Mr
380 Woodhouse want to be seen with them? Who is he?

And so it goes on. Ben now feels more and more uncomfortable, but he doesn't know why. And Mr Woodhouse is still around. Wherever they are, he turns up. Lawrence must give him their schedule, thinks Ben. He sits down and laughs his tinny laugh and sometimes photographers come in and snap* them. At which point Mr Woodhouse laughs even harder.

Looking back, Ben can't believe how he could have been so stupid, how he didn't realise why Mr Woodhouse wanted the publicity. But then one morning he sees Mr Woodhouse's picture in the local paper and reads

bothering: worrying
snob: person who cares too much about social   or class distinctions
snap: (here) take photographs of

390   what Mr Woodhouse is saying and he realises exactly why he has been
so worried.

Mr Woodhouse is a politician. Well of course he is, Ben thinks, it would
have been obvious to anyone less blind. Sally would have spotted it
immediately. But Sally is in New York, and now Mr Woodhouse has
bought Ben and his friends to promote* his small political party. A
party to the right of the far-right*, a party which says that England
should not be a multicultural nation, a party which says that all ethnic*
minorities should leave the country, a party of hate and abuse. Mr
Woodhouse is its leader and with local* elections coming* up, his

400   picture is everywhere. Ben cannot open a paper without seeing Mr
Woodhouse. And what is worse, there are so many pictures of him and
Mr Woodhouse together. Woodhouse and Ben sitting next to him,
smiling, smiling like an idiot. As if Woodhouse was talking to Ben and
Ben liked what he was saying.

Ben is so angry he could kill Lawrence, but he's equally furious with
himself. As he tells Julie when she comes into the café for her morning
espresso.

"It never occurred* to me that he was a politician," Ben says for the
third time. "I feel as if we've all been tricked."

410   "Didn't you know?" she asks. She looks at her nails and thinks that she
might change their colour, go pinker.

Ben looks at Julie as if he was seeing her for the first time and realises

---

promote: bring to the attention of the
public in order to sell, advertise
far-right: with extreme right-wing views
ethnic minorities: groups of people who
do not come from the same race or culture

as the majority of the population
local elections: elections for local government
officers
coming up: in the near future
it never occurred to me: I didn't realise

that he knows nothing about her, her politics, what she believes in. "I looked up Woodhouse on the Internet ages* ago," she continues.

"And it didn't worry you?" he manages to get the words out. His mouth is dry and foul-tasting*, it feels as if something has died in it.

"It's none* of my business," says Julie, shrugging*. "Anyhow, if you're so upset*, Ben, why don't you go and talk to Lawrence?" Ben is beginning to bore her and she hates being bored.

420 "Well of course I knew about Woodhouse," Lawrence confirms after Ben bursts* into his office. "I told you. We were at school together."

"But why didn't you tell us?" Ben needs to know.

"Would it have made any difference? Why should I? Anyhow, I don't tell you about any of the other products you promote, where they're made, whether it's child labour. I don't pay you to think about any of that. I just pay you to smile and promote the stuff."

"But what Woodhouse says isn't right!" Ben is shouting now. "I don't believe this rubbish about a white* England, and there's my face sitting next to him. My mother could see that picture and think that I was a
430 supporter of Woodhouse and his awful party."

"Well, don't show her the paper then," Lawrence is smiling. Ben is too excitable, he thinks, perhaps he should try and arrange a nice Caribbean assignment* for him, maybe that new aftershave. Lawrence

---

ages ago: a long time ago
foul-tasting: with a horrible taste
none of my business: does not concern me
shrugging: lifting one's shoulders to show indifference

upset: unhappy and angry
bursts into: goes into quickly making a lot of noise
a white England: an England where all the people are white, with no ethnic minorities
assignment: job

knows the marketing director, they go back a long way and she owes* Lawrence a favour.

"But what Woodhouse says is wrong," Ben is still talking. "How could you let yourself be taken in by him?"

"Who says I was taken* in?" Ben is beginning to annoy Lawrence. "Look, you're a beautiful boy, Ben. Don't go and spoil* it all by
440   pretending you can think."

"Have you read this speech?" Ben begins again.

"Of course I have," Lawrence replies. "So Woodhouse can be a bit excessive*, but he's only doing it for the votes* and you have to admit there's some truth in what he says. England is a small island. We can't just let everyone in. There isn't room*."

"You're a member of his party, aren't you?" Suddenly Ben is seeing a different Lawrence, his whole world seems to have changed in one morning.

"Well," Lawrence admits, "yes, I am, but I only joined as a favour to Woodhouse. He and I go back a long way. And you have to admit, Ben
450   that …"

But Lawrence finds he is talking to an open door. Ben has gone, he is halfway down the staircase, aware that he can never work for Lawrence again. Ben has gone home, where he sits down and types a short email to Lawrence, resigning* from the agency.

---

owes Lawrence a favour: in a position to do something for Lawrence because Lawrence has done something for her
taken in: deceived
don't go and spoil it: do not ruin the situation

excessive: does or says too much
for the votes: so that people will vote for him
room: enough space
resigning: leaving a job

After sending the email, Ben sits in his Docklands flat, exhausted and drained*. He has acted instinctively and now, as he paces* the floor like a caged animal, he realises that he has spent several years avoiding serious thought. He tries to remember when he last did something because he believed in it or really wanted to do it, but it's too long ago.

460   It's as if he has been half-asleep for the past few years. It was the money, he reflects, it was all too easy. When money comes to you so easily, you take it and keep quiet. You wear the latest designer trainers*, thinks Ben, and you don't ask questions about the workers who make them or how much they are paid or how young they are.

For the first time in years, Ben looks at himself and doesn't like what he sees. He looks around at the London that he thought was so cool, so pleasant, and he likes it even less. So, that's it, he tells himself, it's time for a change.

He writes Sally the longest email he has ever written and tells her what
470   has happened.

"I don't know what I want to do next," he ends, "but I know that with you, whatever I do will be better. Would you think of coming back and starting again with me?"

"Only someone as dumb* as you," emails Sally, "wouldn't see that I love you and I've always loved you. The main reason I went to New York was to get away from the person you'd become, a person who thought that a lifestyle could be a substitute for a life."

---

drained: very tired with no energy
paces: walks backwards and forwards

trainers: sports shoes
dumb: stupid; foolish

480 After Sally comes back, Ben sells his Docklands apartment and together they buy a small pub on the Suffolk coast, not so very far from where Ben grew up. He remembers how much he had always loved the coast there with its wide-open skies and long shingle* beaches.

Running the pub is hard work, but Sally and Ben are sure it's going to be a success. The locals* like the fact that the pub has hardly changed and the weekenders* like the improved food and the live* music. They don't make a lot of money, but it's enough to live on. And, as Sally sometimes says, if they need a bit of extra publicity*, there's always word of mouth.

shingle: made of small stones
locals: people who live nearby
weekenders: people who visit for the weekend (often from towns and cities)

live music: with real musicians, not recorded
publicity: something said or done to attract customers

After Reading

Response

(A) Were you surprised by the ending of the story? Why/why not?

(B) Imagine what Ben wrote to Sally in his long email.
Then write the rest of her reply.

(C) Imagine a conversation between Lawrence and Pete and Julie after Ben has left London. What do you think they say about Ben? Why?

Comprehension

(A) Why do you think people want to look like Ben?

Because he's cool.	
Because they like him.	
Because he's famous.	
Because they want to be like him.	

(B) How do Ben and his friends really feel about Driver's Special and *Tin Pan Alley*?

(C) Ben says that you 'can't just go into any bar'. Why not?
Give two reasons.

(D) What is Ben's apartment like? Write T (True), F (False) or D (Don't know) beside the following words.
Give reasons for your answers.

high-ceilinged	
expensive	

modern	☐
cool	☐
old-fashioned	☐
warm	☐

(E) Why do you think Ben tried to impress his Mum when she visited his apartment?

(F) Why did Sally leave London? What reason does Ben give?

(G) Write an email from Julie to her mother, describing what they will do and where they will go when she comes to London.

(H) What is Ben's plan for the *Paradise Bar*? Does it work?

(I) Write down 5 things you know about Lawrence.

(J) What do the models think about Mr Woodhouse? Tick the correct sentences.

He is one of them.	☐
He doesn't fit in.	☐
He has a horrible laugh.	☐
He wears cool clothes.	☐
He's very funny.	☐

(K) Why does Ben feel as if they have all been tricked?

(L) Why does Ben decide to leave London? List his reasons.

Plot and Setting

Ⓐ   The story can be divided into the following four sections. Give a title to each section.

Introduction (line 1 – line 90)
....

Key event (line 91 – line 330)
....

Climax (line 331 – line 453)
....

Conclusion (line 455 – line 487)
....

Ⓑ   Write a short summary of what happens in each section.

Ⓒ   Ben's apartment is contrasted with the place where he grew up. What does his apartment mean to him? Why does he sell it?

After Reading

Theme

Ⓐ One of the themes of *Word of Mouth* is change. Make a list of all the things you can find in the story which change or have changed.

Ⓑ Do you think the story has a moral? What do you think it is?

Narration and Style

Ⓐ The narration switches from first person to third person. What does this change allow the author to do?

Ⓑ Write down one sentence from the story that isn't told from Ben's point of view.

Ⓒ Why do you think the author has chosen to tell the story using present tenses?

Character

Ⓐ Why do you think that Ben is never described physically? What do you think he should look like?

Ⓑ Did your feelings about Ben change as you read the story? Use examples from the text to show different aspects of Ben's character.

Ⓒ Did your feelings about Julie change after she talked about her mother? Does any other part of the story make you feel differently about her?

D   How are Lawrence and Mr Woodhouse introduced to the reader? What specific words or phrases are used to describe them?

Vocabulary work

A   Match the adjectives on the left with their antonyms (opposites) on the right.

cool	sensible
cutting-edge	delicious
lofty	polite
glossy	unknown
famous	cramped
disgusting	permanent
silly	unfashionable
temporary	out-dated
rude	unpolished

B   Find as many expressions as you can in the story to describe things and people that are fashionable.

After Reading

Ask the Author

(A)   What information for the story came from each of these sources?

        Newspaper articles

        Magazine articles

        TV documentaries

(B)   Put the following into the order in which they happen.

Start to research	
Bring in the characters	
Hear a conversation	
Read something in a newspaper	

After Reading

C   Match the sentence openings with the correct endings.

1. I just want to tell a story ...   a. ... think.

2. I use stories to express ...   b. ... many world issues.

3. I feel that being a writer ...   c. ... how I feel about
                                                    the world.

4. I worry about ...   d. ... my stories.

5. I want people to enjoy ...   e. ... that people want to
                                                    read.

6. I like to make people...   f. ... is a responsibility.

D   Read the following statements and put T (True) or F (False)
    after each one.

The author writes the kind of stories she'd like to read.
She writes stories thinking they are for people learning English.
The author's friend looks over her shoulder as she writes.
People who know her well laugh when they read her stories.
She doesn't think of the reader as she writes.

Follow-up

Speaking

Form groups of four and take the roles of Pete, Julie, Ben and
Sally. Imagine that Pete and Julie are visiting Ben and Sally's pub
in Suffolk. Take turns to give the others the latest news and tell
them what you have been doing.

Writing

Imagine you are Ben's mother. Write a letter to a friend telling her
all about your trip to London to visit him.

Or

Imagine you are Lawrence. Write an email to an old friend telling
him about Ben and what you think of him.

Class activity

Design a questionnaire about attitudes to advertising, including
questions on why people choose to buy certain products.
Now carry out a survey and draw up a report showing your results.

SUE LEATHER

Underground

About the Author

Sue Leather started writing when she was at school. As an adult, she has written a variety of material for learners, including stories and six original EFL readers. She has also written a teacher's resource book, as well as numerous articles on methodology for professional journals. Travel inspires her creative writing, as do her other interests: martial arts, cinema and photography. She loves thrillers, and though she sometimes sits down to write a story in a different genre, it is almost always a thriller that comes out.

Ask the Author

This story is about an innocent man who is found guilty of a crime he didn't commit. It is a subject you've written about before. Why does this issue particularly interest you?

I'm really interested in miscarriages of justice. In some cases in the past, when the death penalty was still law in the UK, it meant that the state killed innocent people. Now capital punishment has been abolished, but there are still countless cases in the UK in which innocent people spend years in prison. The case of the Birmingham Six comes to mind, and just recently a man spent twenty years in prison for a murder he didn't commit. The man had a low level of intelligence and at the time had confessed to the police when they questioned him.

I've always thought that incarceration, putting someone in prison, was a most cruel and unusual punishment. I can't imagine being locked up, not having the freedom that I normally enjoy. Once I happened to walk past Durham Jail and I had a physical reaction, almost as if I was going to be sick. So I guess it's one of my greatest fears, to be locked up, not to be able to swim in the sea or take a walk on the beach.

I'm also convinced that imprisonment is not the answer in a very large number of cases. Some countries, like the USA and the UK, have very large numbers of people in prison. Of course dangerous people need to be locked away from society. But wouldn't it be better if the people who weren't dangerous to the public were put on good rehabilitation programmes and taught how to contribute to society?

Did you base the story on any real events?

I'm an avid newspaper reader and I'm addicted to crime stories, so I'm sure I read something in a newspaper which sparked it off. I'm afraid I can't remember exactly what it was. I do remember reading an article some time ago about suicide on the Underground. Then a colleague of mine went to London recently and the tube train was delayed because of someone jumping in front of it. So that got me thinking.

Did you have to do a lot of research for the story?

No, not really. When I read interesting things, like the number of suicides on the Underground, I know they're going to be useful at some point, so I take notes and wait for the story to arrive. I do need to research things like the hierarchy of the Metropolitan Police, or street names. The Internet makes information like that easy to find out.

You seem to know London very well. Have you lived there?

No, I haven't lived there, but I worked there for some time and commuted in and out every day. Also I still visit on a regular basis. I go to places and take notes if I think they might feature in a story.

London seems to be the main character in this story. Did you plan it this way, or did it develop while you were writing it?

The story started with my interest in a dramatic incident – someone jumping under a tube train – and I just took it from there. You're sitting on the tube, thinking about your work, you're in a hurry. The suicide is a kind of inconvenience in your routine. He's just a stranger, he could be some poor guy whose wife has left him, or has lost his job, or who just can't take it any more. But what if somehow you were connected to this person? That's how it started. London is a good backdrop because having so many people, there is always a chance of there being a connection between you and the guy sitting next to you, or the woman who passes you in the street.

Ⓐ   The word *Underground* can mean:
- below the earth
- anti-establishment art, music, etc.
  (e.g. underground newspapers)
- the subway system in London
- a group which operates secretly in opposition
  to the government.

What do you think *Underground* will mean in this story?
Do you think it may have more than one meaning?

Ⓑ   Read the first paragraph of the story. What kind of atmosphere is
the author trying to create?

Ⓒ   In this story you will meet a detective, a doctor, a chemist and a
builder. Work in groups and discuss what different situations could
bring these characters together.

Ⓓ   Read the following words. Which of them provide a mainly visual
image and which are related to sound?

	SIGHT	SOUND
deserted		
storm		
thunder		
footsteps		
screech		
sea		
scrubbed		
dazed		

Underground

It was the morning rush* hour at Finsbury* Park Underground*
station. For a brief moment between trains, the Victoria line platform
was quiet, almost deserted apart from a few late schoolchildren and
early shoppers. Then suddenly, the calm gave way to the storm. It
started with the thunder of footsteps on the concrete floor, followed by
the screech* of the train as it emerged from the tunnel. Finally, what
seemed like a sea of commuters from Wood Green and Turnpike Lane*
flowed through the arches and onto the platform. Many were dressed in
the unmistakable uniforms of those who work in the City: there were
10 scrubbed* young men in blue suits with yellow ties, older men in grey
or pinstripe* suits with conservative* ties and women in dark-coloured
trouser suits. At this time of the morning they all had the dazed*, blank
look of a herd of cattle going to slaughter*. The dazed look of dreamers
who had been woken too early and not had enough time to get used to
the light before they were plunged* back into underground darkness.

They got onto the train by instinct*, pushing forward into as
comfortable a position as they could. There was no eye contact between
them, no acknowledgement* of each other; that was for later in the day
when they got to the office, when they would briefly become human
20 again. Some scrambled* for the last available seats. The unlucky ones
clung onto the metal poles attached to the ceiling, took out folded
newspapers and scanned the headlines. They struggled to hold onto

---

rush hour: the busy time when people go to
and from work
Finsbury Park: a district in North London
Underground: the subway; London's
underground rail network, also called the Tube
screech: high unpleasant sound, here made
by brakes of the train
Wood Green and Turnpike Lane: London
Underground stations
scrubbed young men: young men with
clean and fresh faces
pinstripe: dark material with thin white vertical
line (often used for suits)
conservative: in a traditional style
dazed: confused, unfocused
slaughter: be killed
plunged: forced down
by instinct: by natural reaction, without thinking
acknowledgement: greeting, recognition
scrambled: moved quickly

their personal space as the carriages became more crowded. Then they settled in to wait for the familiar shuffle* and clatter as the train moved off.

But the train did not move. There was a pause. The commuters fidgeted*. This break in their routine made them feel uncomfortable at some subliminal* level. Minutes passed by. Then there was the sound of the public announcement system crackling* into gear. The voice when it came was male, unmistakably Caribbean.

30

"We apologise for the delay to the Underground train now standing at Finsbury Park. This is due to an obstruction* on the track between Finsbury Park and Highbury and Islington*."

Detective Inspector Dave King, sitting in the third carriage, heard the announcement, folded his newspaper, looked at his watch and sighed. A quarter to nine already. It was always like this on the Tube these days, damn it. He had an appointment with the Deputy Commissioner at 9:30 at New Scotland Yard* and he'd left his home in Tottenham Hale in plenty of time to be there. But you never knew what might happen on the Underground.

40

"An obstruction on the track"… it's bound to be a suicide*, he thought gloomily*. He'd read an article a couple of months ago in the National Police Journal about suicide on the London Underground. According to the article, the most popular station for it was King's Cross.

---

shuffle and clatter: (here) sounds made by the train as it starts to move
fidgeted: moved about restlessly in their seats
subliminal: unconscious
crackling into gear: (here) electronic sounds made by the system being turned on
obstruction: something blocking the track

Highbury and Islington: a north London Underground station
New Scotland Yard: the headquarters of the Metropolitan Police, London's police force
suicide: someone who kills themselves
gloomily: expecting something bad to happen

Underground

There had been an interview with a Tube train driver, King remembered. The driver said they called it a "one-under" and it was the thing that worried them most about their job. Well, you could understand why, he thought. Imagine driving along through a tunnel and then suddenly someone jumping out in front of you in the dark.

50   Imagine the thud* as you hit him ... or her. He shuddered*. Even after all his years in the police, he still found dead bodies hard to deal* with.

He straightened his tie for the umpteenth* time that morning and nervously smoothed down his thinning dark hair. He looked at his reflection in the grimy* window on the opposite side of the carriage. He might be losing his hair a little, but his good looks hadn't quite left him, he thought. Not bad, not bad at all for a forty-five-year-old. Then he looked at his watch again; it was 8:57. He took out his phone which was connected to Scotland Yard. He rang and asked to speak to the Deputy Commissioner's secretary.

60   "Mary, can you tell the governor* I'll be a bit late?" he said. "There's a delay on the Tube."

He put his phone back into the inside pocket of his dark blue suit jacket and stared out at the platform, where there were still some commuters waiting. Behind their vacant* faces a poster urged* the travelling public to visit the south-west of England. The poster showed a picture of the rocky coastline of Cornwall, all sandy coves* and bright sunlight.

---

thud: sound made by a falling object
shuddered: moved his body in disgust
deal with: relate to; work with
umpteenth: more than can be counted
grimy: dirty and greasy

governor: boss (often used in talk when speaking of a superior)
vacant: empty; without emotion
urged: strongly encouraged
coves: small bays; isolated beaches

"Cornwall – beauty and myth" it proclaimed*. Dave King read the words without really registering* them. He shifted* in his seat; he hated being late.

70 At 5:30 that same evening Dave King left New Scotland Yard and walked quickly towards the Tube at St. James's Park, smiling to himself. He'd had a really excellent day. "Good job, Dave," the Deputy Commissioner had said, shaking his hand, "very good job. There'll be a Chief Inspector's job coming up next year, you know. I expect you'll go for it."

Dave was pleased. "Thank you sir," he said, "I must say I enjoy my work with the CID* and I'd really like to carry on". He paused, watching the Deputy Commissioner carefully, trying to measure his reaction. "And I'm quite keen* to get more responsibility." He might as well say it, he thought. "After all, I'm only forty-five … I've still got another fifteen years to go before retirement." There was still plenty of
80 time to make his mark*, even become Detective Superintendent, though he didn't say this to the Deputy Commissioner.

The rest of the day Dave had worked on a tobacco smuggling* case with his colleague Julia Simmons and it seemed they were finally getting somewhere. If they could make progress on this one, reflected Dave, the promotion would be even more likely. Yes, it had been an excellent day all round.

At the news-stand just outside the Underground station, he bought the *London Evening Standard* as usual and went down the steps towards the District and Circle Line. A train arrived almost immediately and he

---

proclaimed: announced
registering: noticing; (here) connecting what he reads to his brain
shifted: moved
CID: Criminal Investigation Department, the

detective branch of the British police force
keen to: interested in; anxious to
make his mark: become successful; make others aware of his abilities
smuggling: bringing goods into a country illegally

90   travelled the one stop to Victoria. There he changed to the Victoria Line
      for the train which would take him towards Tottenham Hale* and
      home. He opened the *Evening Standard* and started reading the sports
      pages. He was happy to see that his team, Spurs, were doing well; they'd
      beaten Manchester United 3-0 last night. All he seemed to read these
      days was the football on the back pages of the newspaper. The rest was
      just bad news and he got enough of that at work.

      As the train was approaching Finsbury Park, he suddenly remembered
      the delay that morning, the "obstruction on the track." It would
      probably be somewhere in the newspaper. He looked back through the
100   pages of the *Standard*. Yes, here it was, on page four: a short report
      under the headline "Bates murderer in death* leap drama." King read
      the report.

      "During this morning's rush hour a man threw himself under an
      Underground train. The incident happened between Finsbury Park and
      Highbury and Islington just before nine o'clock. Police later confirmed
      that the man was Fred Mason (55)."

      "Fred Mason…Mason… I'm sure I know that name," thought King.
      He read on.

      "Mason was killed instantly. A statement issued by the Metropolitan
110   Police confirmed that Mason left Parkhurst Prison one month ago. He
      was released after serving* a twenty-year prison sentence. In 1980, in
      one of the most famous cases of the day, Mason was convicted and sent
      to prison for the murder of Doreen Bates. Mason had always claimed
      his innocence."

Tottenham Hale: a London Underground station   jumping to their death
death leap drama: drama caused by a person   **serving … sentence:** time spent in prison

"Yes, that was it," thought King, "the Doreen Bates murder." King had been a young police officer in the East End of London when it happened. He hadn't really been involved in the case, but he remembered that some of his colleagues had worked on it. He had a vague* memory that it had caused quite* a stir at the time. Some scandal or other, he remembered; there were mutterings* internally
120 about a cover-up*. They always had to get a quick result in high-profile* cases, he thought, and that's when they made mistakes. It wasn't the first and it wouldn't be the last.

"Scotland Yard would not comment," he read, "but local sources say that police had recently questioned Mason." Yes well, he thought, it was common for ex-cons* to get questioned by the police. If a crime happened, first thing you did was check on the ex-cons. He read on. "Dr Vernon James, a psychologist at the Queen Elizabeth Hospital in Westminster said, 'People who leave prison after such a long time often find it very hard to settle back into society. After the initial feeling of
130 delight at being free, they may realise that everything they knew has changed and they can feel totally lost. They often find that they've lost their family and friends. It's not unusual for such people to commit* suicide.' Last year there were a hundred and four suicides. In the five days since the beginning of this year there have already been three."

Sad, thought King, folding his newspaper and preparing to get off the train, after all those years in prison. His mind turned to what he was

vague: faint; unclear
quite a stir: excitement or discussion
mutterings: rumours; unofficial words
cover-up: attempt to prevent information being made public

high-profile cases: legal actions familiar to the public, often because of newspaper coverage
ex-cons: former convicts/prisoners
commit suicide: kill themselves

having for dinner and his regular Tuesday evening game of squash* with his brother. He'd beat him tonight.

Later that evening, Dave King walked round the corner to meet his brother Jack at the Tottenham Squash Club. The brothers were at about the same level, and they both liked to play hard and fast. Jack was a doctor. He was five years younger than Dave and he was lithe* and athletic. The younger man's speed around the court meant that Dave had to work hard to keep up. Dave always enjoyed their games; they kept him fit. He was discovering that that was vital as you got older.

"Fancy* a pint?" Dave asked his brother after they'd showered. The two brothers almost always had a beer in the club bar after the game. "My round," he smiled. It was their ritual that whoever lost paid for the beers.

The Tottenham Squash Club bar was busy as usual, but the brothers managed to find a couple of padded leather seats in the quietest part, near the window. They sat down, sipped their lagers* and started talking about their week. Dave suddenly remembered the incident on the Underground and the report in the newspaper.

"Hey," he said, "I was in your neck of the woods* this morning … there was a jumper* on the Tube."

"What? A suicide?" asked Jack.

---

squash: fast sport played with rackets in an indoor court
lithe: able to bend and move easily
fancy a pint?: Would you like a pint of beer?

lagers: light beers
your neck of the woods: in your neighbourhood/area
jumper: someone who jumps

Dave nodded.

Dave's brother looked sympathetic. "Ugh*, nasty," he said.

160 "Yeah," said Dave, "Then I read later that it was a guy called Fred Mason ... he'd just been released from Parkhurst. Really sad case ... spent all that time in prison and then he goes and does* himself in."

"What did you say his name was?" asked his brother.

"Mason, Fred Mason." said Dave. "Why, was he one of your patients?"

"No, not one of mine, but the name does ring a bell* ..."

The subject changed to football and Dave's possible promotion. After their beer, they left the squash club to go home with Dave promising to beat his brother the following week.

"Get ready for next week," he said, laughing, "because I'm going to
170 thrash* you."

"Yeah, yeah," Jack replied, smiling broadly and turning towards his Volkswagen Golf.

Jack King drove out of Tottenham. At this time of night, he thought, this part of London looked like a wasteland*, litter everywhere and walls covered in graffiti. It took him about twenty-five minutes to get to his semi* in Finsbury Park. Jack worked as a GP* in the area, in a surgery*

---

ugh: sound of disgust
does himself in: kills himself
ring a bell: remind me of something
thrash: beat
wasteland: desolate, ugly and sad location

semi: semi-detached; house joined to the one next door
GP: General Practitioner; a doctor working in the community, i.e. not in a hospital
surgery: (here) clinic where doctors practise

he shared with three other doctors, on Seven Sisters Road. He'd been there for the past eight years. Like most London surgeries, it was very busy, even hectic at times. The waiting room was constantly full of people and there always seemed to be a crisis of some sort. Still, he loved it, thrived* on it. Like his brother, Jack liked to feel that he was making a difference to people's lives.

The next morning he went into the surgery as usual at eight-thirty. He saw a string* of people with flu* or backache and then a frantic mother with a little boy who had a very high temperature. The mother was convinced it was meningitis and was quite hysterical and, in case she was right, he'd had to arrange for the child to be sent to hospital immediately for tests. By eleven o'clock he was more than ready for his coffee break. When he got to the small room where the doctors took their breaks, Dr Tricia Samuels was there, too.

Tricia Samuels was in her thirties. She had been born in Finsbury Park and had grown up there, but her family had originally come from Jamaica. She'd joined the surgery about a year earlier as a partner. Jack liked her a lot. She was a good addition to the surgery, he thought, one of those really caring doctors. And always smiling, too, which helped.

"Hi Tricia, how's it going?" he asked, reaching for the jar of Nescafé from the shelf.

"Oh, okay, you know, the usual," she replied, with a big grin, "flu, flu and more flu!"

"Yeah, me too. It's that time of year," Jack said, sinking down into the next armchair with his coffee.

---

thrived: lived well, happily
string of: a number of

flu: influenza

Then, remembering his conversation with Dave the evening before, he asked "Hey, isn't Ida Mason one of your patients?"

"That's right," she said.

"I thought she was," said Jack, " It was her husband who died yesterday, wasn't it? … that suicide on the Tube … the bloke* who was in prison for twenty years."

"That's right … Fred Mason," said Tricia sadly, "it was in the *Evening Standard*. And Sally says *everybody*'s talking about it in the waiting room this morning." Sally was the surgery receptionist. "I mean, they lived locally," she added.

"Sad business," said Jack, shaking his head.

"Yeah, poor guy* … and poor woman," said Tricia. "In fact, I'm going to call round to her this afternoon."

That afternoon, at 3:45, Dr Tricia Samuels walked up the neat path towards the front door of number 36 Farlow Road. Ida Mason was not a woman who went to the doctor's often. In fact, Tricia had only seen her once before, about three months earlier. Mrs Mason had come to the surgery with a backache. She'd been cheerful then, despite her obvious pain, looking forward to her husband's release from prison.

Dr Samuels knocked on the olive green door of number 36. It was opened by a woman of about fifty, with a kind, round face. "You must be the doctor," she said. "I'm Ellen Greaves, Mrs Mason's sister. It was me who rang the surgery."

---

bloke: man   **guy:** man

"Come through doctor," Ellen Greaves went on, and showed her into the living room, where Ida Mason was sitting weeping*. "I'm so glad you've come. I'll go and make a nice* cup of tea," she added and went off towards the kitchen.

Dr Samuels sat down next to Mrs Mason.

230 "He never did it, doctor," said Ida Mason, tears pouring down her cheeks, "that's the worst of it all. I knew my Fred and he never killed no-one."

Mrs Mason looked awful. Her eyes were swollen red, her hair was uncombed and her dressing gown was stained. Her house, though, was clean and tidy. It was as if Ida Mason was determined to stay respectable, in spite of everything. There were pictures of grandchildren on the shelf and a wedding photograph of her and her husband on top of the TV. There they were, Fred and Ida, standing outside the church, looking young and hopeful in their starched* wedding clothes. The doctor thought how amazing it was that she had waited for him for
240 twenty years, that anyone could wait that long. It was a good thing, thought Tricia, that her patient lived near her sister. Mrs Mason had told her that she'd moved to Finsbury Park from the East End so that she could be nearer to Ellen. Ellen Greaves had been Ida Mason's main support during all the years when Fred was in prison.

"There, there, Mrs Mason" said Tricia Samuels, sympathetically. Unlike a lot of family doctors, she didn't mind this kind of house call. For her, it was visits like this which made her job challenging and worthwhile*.

---

weeping: crying
nice cup of tea: common expression for a cup of tea

starched: stiff (by adding starch when washing white clothes)
worthwhile: deserving the effort made

250 She made a note that Ida Mason would probably need sleeping pills to get her through the next few weeks. She would also need some kind of counselling* support.

"He only came out of prison three months ago," continued Mrs Mason. "Oh, I knew he was depressed, really depressed, but I never thought he'd do this!" With that she dissolved* into floods of tears again.

What a pity, thought Tricia Samuels, that Fred Mason hadn't come to the surgery. Perhaps they could have caught him in time.

Mrs Greaves appeared with a pot of tea and three cups on a tray. The teapot and cups were white with red roses, kind of old-fashioned looking, thought Tricia. Probably Mrs Mason's best china.

260 "There, there, dear," Mrs Greaves said to her sister. "Don't get yourself so worked* up. There's nothing you could have done." Then she addressed the doctor: "She's been like this ever since it happened, doctor. I think she needs something to calm her down."

Dr Samuels nodded.

Mrs Greaves poured the tea and handed a cup to the doctor. "Help yourself to milk and sugar, doctor," she said. Then she put her sister's cup on the little table next to her. Mrs Mason left the tea as if she hadn't seen it and continued with her outburst*.

"We've been campaigning* for almost twenty years to clear his name!"

---

counselling support: someone listening and offering advice and help
dissolved into floods of tears: started to cry again
worked up: upset

outburst: sudden expression of grief or anger
campaigning: actions designed to achieve a purpose, to change a law or correct an injustice, to persuade courts of law to review cases

she said, "but Fred was always worried that he'd have to go back. I
mean, he was falsely accused before. Why shouldn't it happen again?
And then when those police officers came round last week … it was all
too much."

"Go back?" asked the doctor.

"Go back to prison I mean," explained Mrs Mason, "They should get
the one who really killed Doreen Bates, that's what I say … yes, but
they'll never do that!" And again the woman broke into sobs*.

Doctor Samuels let her patient cry. She didn't know whether Fred
Mason had deserved his prison sentence or not; that wasn't part of her
job. The only thing she knew was that here was a woman, her patient, in
need of help. She couldn't help feeling, though, that the police could
have behaved more humanely*. Fancy coming round to pester* him
after twenty years in the nick*!

After a while Mrs Mason became calmer. She drank her tea and stared
blankly ahead of her, out of the window.

The doctor wrote out a prescription for some pills to keep her calm and
gave it to Mrs Greaves. "She should take these three times a day for the
next week or so," she said, "and don't hesitate to call me again if you
need anything." Then, as she picked up her bag and moved towards the
door, she said, "I'll see about a counsellor, too."

"Oh, thank you doctor," said Mrs Greaves, "I'll go to the chemist's and
get the pills as soon as my son arrives. I don't really want to leave her on

---

sobs: sounds one makes when crying
humanely: sympathetically

pester: annoy; bother
in the nick: in prison

her own." As she opened the front door for Dr Samuels, she added, "It's good that it's just on the corner."

About an hour later, Ellen Greaves' son, John, arrived. She left him to look after his aunt, put on her coat and went to Black's Chemist, on the corner of Farlow Road. She handed the prescription to the pharmacist, Graham Black, waited a few moments and then went back to her sister's house with the pills.

300   The chemist watched Ellen Greaves leave the shop. She was another customer he'd never seen before. There was no doubt that business was good here, much better than at Spitalfields. This was a really convenient spot to have a chemist's shop. You got all the locals and you got passing trade* too. Yes, it had been the right move.

Graham Black was a tall, greying man of about fifty. Born in the East End, for the past twenty years he'd lived in Spitalfields, where he'd run a chemist's. But the rents there had gone sky high. All those antique shops and art galleries moving there, an old-fashioned business like his didn't have a chance. So he and his wife decided to move to a different part of London.

310   From time to time, on Friday or Saturday evenings, the Blacks went back to Spitalfields. They liked to see their friends there and have a night out. After all, as they always said to each other, there really was nowhere like the East End for a good night out. They always went to The Seven Bells pub on Lamb Street, which was owned by a friend of theirs.

passing trade: shoppers who just happen to be going past the shop, and then come in

On Friday evening, two days after Ellen Greaves' visit to the chemist's, they took the Tube to Liverpool Street and walked through the old Spitalfields Market to The Seven Bells.

"What are you having?" asked Len Chambers, the landlord* of The
320   Seven Bells. "The usual*?"

Graham Black nodded. He drank bitter*, more out of habit than anything; Jo liked the Australian Chardonnay that Len had started keeping.

"It's good to be back," said Graham to Len. The two men went back a long way*.

"Good to see both of you," said Len, raising his glass, "By the way, the Beef Tournedos is first class this evening. The wonderful Michel is on top form."

The Seven Bells had a really outstanding* restaurant. Len Chambers
330   had been clever enough to see ahead of time that Spitalfields was going to be one of the trendiest* places in London. He'd found a very good French chef, Michel, and despite the fierce competition in the area, the pub was still as popular as ever.

The bar, as with any weekend night, was jam-packed*. The crowd was a good mix of locals, the old East-Enders, and newcomers: young stockbrokers, computer analysts* and graphic designers*. The Blacks

---

landlord: owner of a pub, hotel, etc.
the usual: the drink you usually have
bitter: British dark beer
went back a long way: had known each other for a long time
outstanding: excellent

trendiest: most fashionable
jam-packed: extremely full
computer analysts: people who work studying computers and computer systems
graphic designers: people who create designs for posters, books or magazines

sat at a small table not far from the bar. There were two middle-aged men sitting at the next table, just a foot or so away. One was speaking energetically, while the other listened. The speaker looked scruffy*; he wore a greasy striped tie and badly needed a shave. The listener was about the same age, late forties, but clean-shaven* and well dressed. Despite the noise in the bar, it wasn't hard to hear their conversation.

"My Doreen wasn't like that, Bob," said the scruffy man to the other. "All those things they said in court and in the papers about Doreen having affairs* with all those men! It wasn't true. She was an angel, that woman!"

Graham Black looked at his wife meaningfully, nodding his head towards the next table, indicating that she should try to listen to the conversation. Jo Black looked towards the table, trying not to make it obvious that she was looking.

"Bloody newspapers!!" the scruffy man went on angrily. He was getting really steamed* up. "Well, I'm glad Mason's topped himself*. Should have done it years ago, as far as I'm concerned. They should never have let him out of prison. There's no doubt in my mind that he killed her, Bob, no doubt at all. Bloody maniac*!!" His companion listened without saying anything. The expression on his face showed that he had heard it all before.

"Table's ready!" called Len. The Blacks got up, a little regretfully, and went to the restaurant for dinner, whispering about the conversation they'd overheard.

---

scruffy: untidy and dirty
clean-shaven: without a beard
affairs: sexual relationships with other people when one has a partner

steamed up: angry
topped himself: killed himself
maniac: madman

The man with the greasy tie, Des Bates, carried on talking for a few minutes, then paused for breath. His companion, Bob Jenkins, jumped* in and said, "Yeah, well, Fred Mason's gone now, mate*. Best thing, as you say. Fancy another drink?"

Bob Jenkins got up and went to the bar to get the beers, thinking about what Des had said. He'd heard it all before of course. Doreen Bates! An angel!! Of course he hadn't said anything to Des – and he never would – but everyone knew that Doreen had had quite a few affairs in her time. It had even been murmured that one of her special friends had been someone quite important. Yeah, everyone knew that Doreen was no angel – except Des! Oh she'd been all right, thought Bob, nice enough in her way, and really pretty, but everybody knew she'd been making a fool of Des. Didn't deserve to be murdered, of course. Who does? But an angel … !!

"Two pints, please Len," Bob said to the landlord, putting the empty beer glasses on the bar.

"Coming up," Len replied, "How's business?"

"Oh, you know, pretty good," said Bob.

"Good," said Len, putting the two foaming* pints of bitter on the bar. "Listen, I was wondering if you could come and start the extension to the cellar next week?"

Bob Jenkins was a builder. He had his own little construction company

jumped in: interrupted
mate: friend; friendly way of addressing a man
foaming: topped with a layer of white bubbles

just off Mile End Road, and had three men who worked for him. He did very well in the area. His work was good and he was always in demand. People always needed extensions to their houses, lofts*, garages, that kind of thing. He wasn't exactly rich, but he liked to think of himself as "comfortably off*."

"No problem, mate," he said, "I'm off to do a big job over in Richmond next week, but I'll send Matt over. He'll get it done in three days, I
390 should think."

"Richmond is it?" said Len, admiringly, "You must be doing pretty well for yourself!!"

Bob smiled. Yes, Jenkins Builders was doing well. Richmond was one of the posher* parts of London and Bob Jenkins had been asked to do a roofing job on a really big house belonging to a barrister. The barrister had heard of Jenkins through a friend of a friend. Well, you couldn't say "no" to a job like that. It was going to be a five-day job, eight-hours a day for two men. Bob would take his mate Joe Raglan with him. Yeah, Bob was going to make a pretty penny* out of that. Enough to take his
400 wife Julie on a second holiday to Majorca, perhaps.

"Yeah," he laughed and gave Len the thumbs up gesture, "we're on the up and up*, mate."

Early on Monday morning, Bob and Joe went off to Richmond in Bob's Bedford van to start work on the barrister's roof. The house was a

lofts: attics; spaces under the roof of a house, often converted to make extra rooms
comfortably off: with enough money for a comfortable life
posher: richer and more exclusive
pretty penny: significant amount of money
on the up and up: doing well financially and socially

detached* six-bedroom house in a quiet street. Really nice, thought Bob, just what Julie and me would like. The two men unloaded the van, got ready and went up on the roof.

Within twenty minutes they were hard at work. They worked more or less silently for an hour. Then, suddenly, Joe stopped work and looked around. "Here look at this, Bob," he said, pointing in the direction of another large house. Bob looked. The house was even bigger than the barrister's, with a very large garden on the other side and a conservatory*, built onto the side nearest to the barrister's house.

Conservatories were becoming more and more popular, thought Bob. Well, it was the only way you could grow tropical* plants in England. And most people used them as extra rooms. Much cheaper than moving house. Yes, he would have to start building them himself soon; that would expand his business! Bob peered* into the conservatory and could just see the figure of a grey-haired man, relaxing in a lounge chair. "Lucky devil!" said Bob out loud.

James Barker, retired Chief Superintendent of the Metropolitan Police, relaxed in his conservatory and sipped a cup of tea. He felt satisfied. Why shouldn't he? He'd retired from the force* eight years ago, with an excellent pension. He and his wife Elizabeth had always been careful with money, always saved, so they had quite a nice sum of money in the bank. In fact, they'd been able to buy the house *and* have quite a lot left. Yes, he was enjoying his retirement in what estate agents called "leafy Richmond."

---

detached : single house not joined to another one
conservatory: room, mostly of glass, added to a house as an extra room or to grow plants and flowers
tropical: from hot (tropical) countries
peered: looked intently
force: police force

"Here's the newspaper, dear," said his wife Elizabeth, coming into the
430 conservatory and placing *The Daily Telegraph* down next to his drink.

James Barker put on his reading glasses. He opened the newspaper
lazily and flicked* through it. Nothing much here, he thought, as usual.
Then his eyes fell upon a short article on one of the inside pages.
"Ex-con Tube suicide." Barker started to read with interest.

Barker closed the newspaper quickly.

flicked: looked quickly from page to page

Well, that was for the best, he thought. That was the end of that. Doreen Bates … he'd rather liked Doreen Bates. And Doreen Bates had rather liked him! Oh, just a bit of fun, nothing serious. She was that kind of woman. Very pretty and very silly. And it turned out that it
440 wasn't just him she was having an affair with. Oh no, there were quite a few of them, including a company director and a headmaster … she always seemed to go for* important men in the community.

Problem was that she liked to talk. And talk was dangerous. Well, it didn't look good, anybody could see that. After all, at the time he'd been a Chief Inspector. And he was well known around the East End; that was his special patch*. He was a respected member of the community and a married man. And Doreen had threatened to tell his wife, even the men who worked for him. It was a very dangerous situation. Of course he'd had to get rid of her*.

450 He remembered the night twenty-two years ago when he'd arranged to meet her in that park in Bethnal Green. It was dark, unlit. It was a perfect place for a lovers' meeting. And on that January night there was no-one else there; it was far too cold. He and Doreen Bates always met where nobody could see them, of course, so she had suspected nothing. He'd taken one of his wife's stockings with him and had strangled her with it. It was easy; she was a small woman, a slip of a thing* really, and he was a big man, tall and strong. It had been the easiest thing in the world to stop her making a noise.

He hadn't arrested Fred Mason himself of course; he'd sent one of his
460 men to do it. Fred Mason was the perfect choice; everybody knew that

---

go for: be attracted by
special patch: area where he worked and was known

get rid of her: (here) kill her
slip of a thing: very small and slight

he was a bit simple. And Fred knew Doreen Bates, too. The good thing was that he wasn't exactly bright, Mason. He was the sort of man you could imagine doing something like that. Anyway, everyone believed it; it was easy to get him convicted.

Yes, thought James Barker, as he drank his tea and took off his reading glasses, it was a good thing that Fred Mason had thrown himself under a train on the Underground. It was really all for the best …

After Reading

Response

Ⓐ   Were you surprised by the ending of the story? What kind of ending had you been expecting?

Ⓑ   Do you think there is a main character in the story? If so, who do you think it is? Give reasons for your choice.

Ⓒ   Which character do you like best and why?

Comprehension

Ⓐ   The author uses two comparisons to describe the dazed look of the commuters. What is the effect of these two images? Do you think the similes are successful? Why?

Ⓑ   What is Dave King's attitude or reaction to the following:
    The public announcement
    Dead bodies
    The travel poster
    His appearance
    Being late

Ⓒ   Why did Dave feel "it had been an excellent day all round"?

Ⓓ   Write T (True), F (False) or N (Not known) after the following statements.

    Mason was a murderer.
    Doreen Bates was a murderer.
    Mason was found guilty of murder.
    Mason said he was guilty of murder.

After Reading

> Mason spent twenty years in prison. ▢
> Mason jumped because he was guilty. ▢

(E) When people leave prison after serving a long sentence they often find it hard to settle back into society. Quote three reasons from the text to support this statement.

(F) Why did Dave tell Jack about Fred Mason? Did Jack know him?

(G) Match the words and phrases below to the characters or places.

Jack

The surgery

The mother

Tricia

hysterical

busy

caring

hectic

loved it

smiling

frantic

thrived on it

(H) Find reasons in the text for the following statements about Ida Mason.
"Her eyes were swollen red"
"Her house .... was clean and tidy"
"...she'd moved to Finsbury Park"
"she would also need some kind of counselling support"

After Reading

(I)   Why did Graham Black move and what were the advantages of his new location?

(J)   Find words in the text (from line 330 to line 343) with opposite meanings to the following:

awful	....
stupid	....
most unfashionable	....
empty	....
lazily	....
neat	....
bearded	....

(K)   What was Bob Jenkins' opinion of Doreen Bates? How was it different from Des Bates' view of Doreen?

Plot and Setting

(A)   This story does not develop in a conventional way. Draw a diagram to show how the plot unfolds.

(B)   What do you think is the climax of the story? Is there a conclusion? Do you think the story needs one?

Ⓒ Which character links the following pairs of characters?
For example:

Dave King   Tricia Samuels

The linking character is Jack.

Note that there are two possible answers for the last pair.

Tricia   Graham Black

....

Graham Black   Bob Jenkins

....

Des Bates   James Barker

....

Ⓓ The author describes Mrs Mason's house in detail. How does the
setting add to the reader's understanding of her character?

Theme

Ⓐ When someone is convicted of a crime they did not commit it is
called a miscarriage of justice. Read what the author says about
this subject on page 44. Is it the same as the attitudes to the
issue expressed by the characters in the story?
How does it differ? Give examples.

(B)   Read the alternative titles below.
Which do you think best fits the story and why?

City of Strangers
The Wrong Man
Jumper
On the Move

(C)   Class activity: brainstorm other titles for the story.

Narration and Style

(A)   The story is told both from the narrator's point of view and the characters' points of view. Why do you think the characters' points of view are important in this story? Give examples.

(B)   The following sentences are in standard English. Find colloquial versions of them in the text.
For example: Would you like a glass of beer? is "Fancy a pint?"

I was near where you live this morning
Don't get so upset
I'm glad that Mason killed himself
You must be prospering
Yes, everything is getting better and better

(C)   How does the author use time and references to time to give an impression of life in a big city?

After Reading

Character

Ⓐ Which character is described in most detail? Explain why.

Ⓑ Why do you think the author decided not to develop individual characters within the story?

Ⓒ Write a description of Fred Mason as seen by two different characters in the story.

Vocabulary work

Ⓐ Match the words below to form phrases used in the text.

personal	job
quick	memory
subliminal	space
public	move
dead	result
vague	bodies
high	competition
right	announcement
fierce	level
big	temperature

Ⓑ Make a list of all the professions and jobs mentioned in the story and write a short explanation of what each one entails.

Ask the Author

Ⓐ Match the following words or phrases with the correct definitions.

miscarriage of justice	admitted to a crime
capital punishment	being locked up in prison
abolished	being trained to live a crime-free life
incarceration	the death penalty
confessed	when someone is wrongly convicted
rehabilitation	brought to an end

Ⓑ Which of the following did the author research? Tick all the correct answers.

Crime stories

Street names

Suicides on the Underground

The hierarchy of the Metropolitan Police

Tube train delays

Ⓒ Read the following statements and tick T (True) or F (False).

	T	F
The author has lived in London.		
The author commuted in and out of London every day.		
The author often visits London.		
The author doesn't visit places just because they are going to be in a story.		

Ⓓ   Choose the correct answer.

The story began with:
> the author's interest in drama.

> a suicide.

> a routine incident.

London is a good backdrop because:
> you know the person sitting next to you.

> it has a huge population.

> you are connected to so many people.

Follow-up

Speaking
Class activity. What happens next?
Begin by saying: "Dave King was sitting in an Underground train one morning . . ."
Each student in turn narrates what happens next.

Writing
Write an article for a newspaper telling the true story of Fred Mason.

Or

Design a campaign poster to help clear Fred Mason's name.

Class activity
Stage a class debate on the positive and negative aspects of living in a big city, using some of the examples of city life described in the story. For example you might want to mention restaurants or sports clubs as positive and busy doctors' surgeries and dirty streets as negative.

J A N E   S P I R O

Travelling
Light

About the Author

Jane Spiro is a teacher trainer, language teacher, materials writer, presenter for local TV, and writer of poetry, fiction and plays. She has published four influential papers on the testing of literature, two collections of short stories for language learners (*The Place of the Lotus* and *The Twin Chariot*), language tests for Cornelsen Verlag (*Highlight 6*), a novel (*Nothing I Touch Stands Still*), and is working on a creative writing resource book for Oxford University Press. She is currently Senior Lecturer at Oxford Brookes University where she runs an MA in English Language Teaching.

Ask the Author

What inspired you to write this story?

There were several sources of inspiration for this story. The first was the experience of moving house, which I have done many times. Each time, a removals man has come in, brisk and unemotional, and emptied out the house. I would often wonder what he thought, seeing the place I was leaving and where I was going to. It seemed to be one of those jobs, like an estate agent or a lawyer, where you are meeting people on the point of change. I've often thought that these journeys are a rich source of stories. Who is moving and why? Where are they moving to and where from?

A second source of inspiration for the story was holidays I had in my early twenties, hitch-hiking around Europe and driving in a van right through to Istanbul. It made me aware of the magic of the road, the late-night and early-morning hours when you have a single purpose: to reach a destination. And the road itself is quite hypnotic, you almost seem to be in an alternative universe.

Another source of inspiration was a school reunion, about ten years after we had left school. What amazed me was how instantly and intensely the old feelings were evoked; the girls (it was an all-girls school) who had made me feel second-rate and dowdy still made me feel the same way. The girls who had had a brightness and excitement about them still did. Just the same, there were feelings of envy and inferiority, even though now I have fulfilled many of my dreams and am very happy with my choice of lifestyle. This, too, made me think about how our emotions can get caught in the past and how something quite unexpected can catapult our feelings right back in time, to a state we thought was long forgotten.

Have you travelled much?

Yes, my student holidays gave me a taste for travel that I have never recovered from. After exploring Europe on very little money, always on the edge of everyday life, staying in hostels and meeting other travellers, I became determined to travel for a purpose. In a way that allowed me to meet local people, enter their homes and understand their language. Since then, the profession of English language teaching has taken me to five continents, to Mexico, Kenya, Egypt, India, Sri Lanka and Japan. It has also given me the opportunity to live and work in parts of Europe that had been unknown to me, such as Hungary, Poland, Romania, the Czech Republic and Russia. I have spent days on the road, just like Len in the story. In 1991 I packed up my household and drove from Nottingham to southern Hungary, all night along the frighteningly fast German motorways, and narrow potholed Hungarian back roads. For years, too, I had a fascination with India, and worked and travelled wherever I could go safely: from Tamil Nadu in the tip, to the foothills of the Himalayas. I have been to most of the places Len talks about, and share with him the sense of privilege at being there.

Which of the two main characters do you identify with most?

The two men, George and Len, are both aspects of myself. In fact, in developing the story, I was really exploring this dilemma in myself: the contrast between the pleasure of having a home, and the urge to explore and be an adventurer. Choosing one and not the other is always a sacrifice. Having a home gives you the most marvellous sense of calm and rootedness. I have understood only recently what it is like to plant roses, and see them grow from a sprig and wind themselves around the trellis. And yet that means giving up the idea of 'travelling light': being able to uproot and go. And of course the reverse is true: the eternal traveller will never see the sprigs grow into yellow roses.

This is also true of the people around you. For years, while I was travelling, I was developing friendships that were pulled apart, that came and went. Here you are in a world where no-one has known you for very long. That's exciting, in a way, because you can always reinvent yourself, as Len does. But George is telling the opposite story: just how deeply nourishing it is to be with people with whom you share a past, people who won't just disappear.

George and Len are, of course, extreme examples of each case, and I think my own resolution has been to be a little bit of both George and Len most of the time, at least as far as that's physically possible!

You've recently published a novel. What do you think is the main difference in writing a short story and a novel?

This short story might be one episode in a novel. The key focus I had in writing the novel was the overall drive of the characters; and the characters in turn drove the plot. I wanted to show not only how one character changed over time, but how two characters in two different periods, mirrored and echoed one another. This entailed a whole cluster of episodes, insights and interactions. The short story in a way telescopes all these together. One episode serves to do everything – to reveal character, to demonstrate change – even tiny and subtle change, and to say something about characters echoing and mirroring one another. I suppose a short story is like a haiku: it reveals a subtle moment of change, which may be symbolic of something bigger – but in itself is delicate, almost imperceptible. A novel, on the other hand, is like an epic – the moment of change is fully contextualised. You show all the hundred and one factors which lead up to it, and which lead away from it.

Before Reading

Ⓐ   Which of the following is correct?
Travelling light means travelling:

       during daylight hours.   ☐
       with very little luggage.   ☐
       in a balloon.   ☐

Titles often have more than one meaning.
Can you think of a metaphorical meaning for travelling light?

Ⓑ   Read the first sentence. Imagine this is a story you are writing. What would you add to the description? Think about the weather, the look of the streets and what people might be wearing.

Ⓒ   The main characters in the story are a long-distance lorry driver and a taxi driver. In what ways do you think their lives will be different?

Travelling Light

An afternoon in November, 16:30 and the lights are on in London.

It had grown darker and darker as Len travelled north through Europe. Crete was all white rooftops and the smell of crushed figs. Hungary was dark red, with cherry trees and ripe vines. Then the grey and silver of German motorways. On the German motorways you moved fast, acted fast, and the rain was silver . . .

Now in November it was England with sky like mud, and he was stuck. The London traffic was going nowhere. Rain, smudging* under the windscreen* wipers, leaving the windscreen brown.

10   "Only London rain is this colour," Len thought. "Dirtiest rain in Europe."

He hadn't been irritated in Crete when the police searched every inch of his lorry. He hadn't been irritated in Hungary when another lorry pushed him off the road. But in London he was irritated because this is where he was born. Somehow you expect the place where you're born to be well-behaved. And London wasn't. It was messy. Perfectly nice streets had developed road bumps* and bollards* that narrowed them. Roads you could once go up and down had changed direction and developed *No Entry* signs. When you needed a garage, there were only
20   furniture warehouses*; when you needed a lay-by^, there were only expensive car parks or *Park and Ride*^ bus yards.
"Glad I left," he thought. "Glad I'm always on the move."

---

smudging: making a dirty mark
windscreen wipers: blades with rubber edges
that clear rain from car windscreens
road bumps: raised areas made to slow cars
down
bollards: posts to stop cars driving on the
pavement
furniture warehouses: large furniture shops
lay-by: area just off a road where cars can stop
Park and Ride **bus yards:** car parks where
motorists can leave their cars and take buses
into the centre of a town

ECCLES REMOVALS - Long distance transport and delivery anywhere in the world read the sign on his lorry. Len was proud. He could so easily have stayed at home and worked in his dad's garage and gone nowhere. But instead he had his name in letters one metre high on the side of his rig* and his great wheels had rolled across dozens of borders. In Len's world, everyone was like him: in transit*. It suited him fine. He had moved a banker from a Birmingham suburb to a farm in Andalusia, a

30   family from a walnut farm in Turkey to an apartment block in Munich, he had moved two harps and a grand piano* from Naples to Nairobi, and now he had moved a homesick* Englishman from his villa in Crete back to England. He knew the beginnings of hundreds of stories, people leaving, people arriving, people in transit with their furniture and books and musical instruments, boxes of letters and photographs, children's cots* and toys. Hundreds of beginnings, but never the endings.

But now the traffic had trapped him and he wasn't moving anywhere. He was stuck. He was crawling* so slowly he could look into the windows of the houses along the road. Some were already decorated for Christmas,

40   with tired-looking paper reindeer* hanging on strings and lines of broken fairy* lights, like blind eyes around doorways. Sad patches of grass were trying to be gardens: prickly*, mean-looking* bushes leeched* to walls, dead roses hung crumpled off trellises*, the odd dried-out fish pond was still decorated with hopeful rocks and a dusty gnome*.

rig: formerly American name for a lorry or truck
in transit: on the move
grand piano: concert-size piano
homesick: feeling of missing one's home
cots: beds with high sides for babies and young children
crawling: (here) going very slowly
reindeer: deer from Arctic regions associated with Father Christmas (Santa Claus)
fairy lights: small lights used to decorate Christmas trees
prickly: covered with prickles (sharp points)
mean-looking: (here) aggressive (because they are covered with prickles)
leeched: clinging on
trellises: open fences used for climbing plants
gnome: garden statue of a little old man

The only signs of life were virulent* beds of weeds that had taken hold of lawns, or had bedded themselves into the cracks of walls and were pulling them apart.

Then the houses gave way to a parade* of shops: a dressmaker's shop with faded ball* gowns in the window, a betting* shop, a frozen food
50　shop and a boarded-up* army surplus* shop daubed with graffiti. Not a single shop where he'd want to buy anything, Len reflected.

In Crete, while he was packing up the house, he had begun chatting to the Englishman who had tried to start a new life running a trinket* shop for tourists. It hadn't worked. The tourists hadn't been interested in an Englishman selling them souvenirs and the Englishman hadn't been interested in learning Greek. His wife had been miserable and her misery had infected* him, too. They began to pull each other into a nostalgia* for their life back home. He got homesick, missed his old school friends. He had told Len this, with the light white on the
60　rooftops and the Mediterranean like a blue pearl below. It was one of the stories Len just couldn't understand. How on earth could you be miserable with sea and sunlight and the smell of fresh figs? Why on earth would you choose London over that?

Len himself had forgotten what it was like to miss anywhere or to want to be in one place rather than another. Where you were was where you wanted to be. That was the only way you could manage. When he

virulent: dangerous or harmful
parade: row
ball gowns: long dresses worn to formal parties and dances
betting shop: where one can gamble on horse races or other sports
boarded-up: closed with its windows covered

over to prevent them from being broken
army surplus shop: shop selling old army supplies e.g. uniforms
trinket: cheap souvenir or other ornament
infected: spread to
nostalgia: longing; desire for something from your past

stayed in motels or slept in his truck by the side of a road, what was the point of wanting to be near old friends? None! They would have long forgotten him. Did he ever think about childhood or schooldays when
70　every day he had a new journey to complete? Never! Did he ever think about Carla whom he had left behind in Rome, or Aysha whom he had left behind in Istanbul? No! They were in the past. Did he want to go back to the place where he grew up? Never! And as for homesick – well first you have to have a home to be sick about. "Glad I don't have that kind of sickness," Len thought.

The truck was the home that he loved: Gloria he'd called her. She had been more faithful and true to him than all the women he had met. Gloria had red velvet curtains and a leather seat which folded down into a bed as comfortable as a dream. In the eerie* dawn light in
80　motorway lay-bys, he would make a cup of tea on his little stove and watch the sunset through Gloria's windows, warm his hands over the stove, slide Marianne Faithfull into his multi-play CD and listen to the music, cradling the cup of tea in his hands. Sometimes the road, the not speaking, was hypnotic*. He would pull into a lay-by, buy a burger and can of beer from the roadside* van, and he could see that the other truckers* were hypnotised*, too. They would stroll around with faces like ghosts in some other world. They didn't need to speak. They would nod at each other, or honk* as they pulled out back onto the road. But sometimes it was quite the opposite: sometimes they were like priests,
90　confessing to each other in the darkness.

Len had said things to other truckers he had never said, even to himself, before. He had wept into his tea, telling one of them about his mother

---

eerie: strange; mysterious
hypnotic: feeling one is about to fall asleep
roadside van: van that sells food at the side of the road

truckers: lorry drivers, usually long-distance
hypnotised: in a semi-conscious state
honk: hoot

who had left him when he was too young to remember, and another had wept into his, telling Len about his passion for a film star who made secret signs to him through the film screen. They understood each other, they were truckers, all-night travellers.

The London traffic edged* forward into a spaghetti* of roads and flyovers*. Len had just done a small job in Harlesden, picking up a huge painted dog kennel*. The dog kennel and the Cretan furniture both had
100 to get to Watford by morning. He reflected on the possibilities for the night: Harry's guesthouse at Crouch* End, but the sheets had been damp* last time he'd stayed there, or the Junction 8 motorway motel, that would be good, but a bit out of his way. Just now, where he was on the North* Circular, his options were open.

In the Watford* direction, there was a long caterpillar of cars. He couldn't see the end of it, and the caterpillar wasn't moving. Then he noticed a road sliding into a tunnel in the other direction. The road was empty and curiously inviting. Not just because there was no traffic, but because it seemed to lure* him in. Drive down me, it said.

110 Len indicated left and pulled out. Now he was moving fast through the tunnel, down the back of some industrial estate and on through back streets, where he loomed* like a huge monster over pedestrians and motorcyclists. A sense of familiarity was beginning to creep over him, maybe because all these London districts looked alike, maybe because these streets were like the ones that appeared in occasional* nightmares

edged forward: moved forward a short distance slowly
spaghetti: twisting shape
flyovers: roads that go over other roads
dog kennel: small house for a dog
Crouch End: district in North London
damp: not dry

North Circular: main road that circles north London
Watford: London suburb
lure: pull; seduce
loomed: suddenly appeared (used of large, often frightening, shapes)
occasional: not regular

of going back to school. There were low familiar houses edged in between unfamiliar blocks of flats in pale brick, and familiar rows of shops suddenly broken by supermarkets glowing in the street lights. It all flashed on and off in his memory like a light bulb - yes, no, yes, no.

120 Is it? Isn't it? - until the roads opened out into a street and a row of high iron railings. It could be the old school, it really could. And then a name jumped out of the lamplight.

Brent Road Boys' School

Blimey*, this didn't just look like his school, this *was* his school, the very one – and just the same as if he had walked out of it yesterday.

He sat at the red traffic lights in his high cab*, but in his mind he was a small boy cycling home on the rusty bicycle he had found abandoned* in the park, looking up at the huge lorry with its big letters: ECCLES REMOVALS. Wow! Long distance. With letters as tall as I am.

130 When the car behind began hooting, it took him some moments to realise that the lights had gone green and that he was the lorry and it was his job to move.

He moved slowly now. He could have drawn the street with his eyes closed. Next to the school the concrete playground surrounded by iron railings*. Then, on the other side of the railings, the Municipal* Baths in red brick and huge windows like a church. Red brick and his bicycle chained to the railings after school. The antique shop with dusty broken sofas in the window, the lingerie* shop where he had seen his first pair

---

blimey: exclamation used to show surprise
cab: the part of the lorry in which the driver sits
abandoned: left behind

railings: metal posts
Municipal Baths: public baths in a town (no longer used in Britain)
lingerie: women's night clothes and underwear

of stockings on a pair of plastic legs, the pet shop which only sold parrot
140   cages and goldfish. Len Eccles had sprung from here. He could not
escape it. London was sucking him back. Stop, it said. Stop and find me.

But now the road itself pushed him on, and he couldn't stop, couldn't
stop at all. He was on automatic now. Pet shop, *Smokey Joe's*, and dad's
garage, Harry Eccles Motor Repairs. Go on, turn in – his past called to
him – just like you used to. He turned into the garage forecourt*. His
great rig, ECCLES REMOVALS, rolled into the garage where he had
grown up.

It was quite normal for a lorry to roll into a garage. There were no
groups of people to greet him with flowers and banners and cheering.
150   As he climbed down from his high seat no-one ran to kiss him, no-one
said: "I remember you as a child! I knew your father, such a kind man!
How you've grown! My*, what a big lorry!"

It was a very quiet way to arrive at a place you hadn't seen for twenty
years. The big messy* workshop, where his dad had climbed under cars
and come out black and smelling of oil, had gone. Instead, there was a
glass-fronted* Safeways garage shop, with rows of potted* plants and a
fridge full of plastic-wrapped sandwiches. The hut where his dad made
himself tea was gone, too. In its place was a car wash with two rollers
like huge orange mops*. No-one climbed under your car or lorry here
160   any more. If your engine fell out, right here on the forecourt, it would be
just too bad. There was no-one here to do anything at all, not even to fill
up your tank as they used to do; only the teenager with a tooth-brace*
who sat behind the till.

---

forecourt: front area of a garage   or shop
my: my goodness   **potted plants:** plants in pots
messy: untidy; dirty   **mops:** tools for washing made of thick string
glass-fronted: glass walls of a supermarket   **tooth-brace:** device used to straighten teeth

Len filled up with diesel*, paid at the machine, then moved his lorry into the side. He could stay there for a while, see if *Smokey Joe's* was still open.

Smokey Joe's was the café next door to Eccles Motor Repairs. This was the place where he had grown up, done his homework – badly – on the plastic tablecloth, stopped doing his homework, met girls, learnt to smoke, drunk his first cup of coffee, discovered Marmite*, brown sauce* and Branston pickle*. Smokey Joe had made him baked beans* on toast for tea, while he waited for his dad to finish work. Smokey Joe had been like a mum might have been, if he'd had a mum who'd stayed, instead of a mum who had gone away. Smokey Joe had a daughter with long brown legs and long brown hair to match; she had white socks with white teeth to match.

He hadn't thought about Smokey Joe and his daughter with the long brown hair for twenty years.

But *Smokey Joe's* had changed its name, and its look, and its menu. It was now *Saucy Sally's* and the menu was all savoury* dips and hot sauces. There was a chilli* sauce, a pesto* sauce, a carbonara* sauce, a black bean sauce, a sweet and sour* sauce and a hot spicy sauce. The tables were all steel with high bar stools. Len felt a bit too old, and too awkward, and too unshaven to sit at one of these cool clean tables. But he did. Just to get the feel of it. Just to pretend it was the old days, back again in the same old place.

170

180

---

diesel: heavy oil used to run lorries
Marmite: savoury spread for bread or toast
brown sauce: traditional British bottled spicy sauce
Branston pickle: brand of cold thick spicy sauce
baked beans: tinned cooked beans in tomato sauce
savoury dips: sauces used for dipping bread or

other foods
chilli: hot pepper
pesto: Italian basil sauce
carbonara: Italian pasta sauce of bacon, egg and cheese
sweet and sour: Chinese sauce

A woman with spiky* blonde hair and dark eyes came out of the
kitchen to take his order.

190 "Yeah, what d'you* want?" she asked, folding over a new page of her
pad. She sounded so like Smokey Joe. "What d'you want today, young
lad*? Beans on toast? Marmite sandwich? Cup of cocoa while you wait
for dad?" he used to say like mums might say. That's what they'd say
after school, when you got back in time for tea.

But the woman with the hair was still waiting.

"I haven't got all day*," she said.

Len pointed at one of the sauces on the menu, without thinking.

"Number 12," she read. "With noodles, rice or tacos*?"

"The first one."

"Noodles. And to drink?"

200 "Beer."

"We're not a pub. Tea or coffee?"

"Cuppa* tea."

spiky: with spikes, points
d'you: do you
lad: boy (here an affectionate way of
addressing the young Len)

haven't got all day: am in a hurry
tacos: Mexican fried pancakes
cuppa: a cup of

She had great legs, Len noticed, as she walked into the kitchen.

Kids at school had thought it was really cool that he had spent his evenings in a café. Most of them thought it was much more fun than spending the evenings at home with their parents. Len as a lad hadn't been so sure. Sometimes there had been times when he'd have liked a home and a mother, instead of just a dad underneath a lorry, and a café with a kind man called Smokey Joe.

210 Some of the kids used to come back to the café with him for tea after school. They'd do that for two, or even three nights. Then they'd get tired of it, and make excuses. The only kid who lasted more than three nights was George Trubshaw. George came to the café with Len every evening for three weeks. Len thought he had made a real friend. He thought George ate beans on toast with him because they liked each other. Then suddenly, George said he was sick of beans. "You can have egg and chips instead," Len told him. But it was no good. George never came again.

Smokey Joe had always noticed. "On your own again, lad?" He would
220 rumple* Len's hair. "Travel light*, lad. Don't let it bother you."

Len was thinking about this, when the door opened and a man came in. He looked confident, relaxed, as if he was a regular visitor. He went straight to the table nearest the kitchen, as if this was his usual place. He had a kind, slightly creased* face with marks round the eyes that made him look as if he was permanently smiling, and his hair was thick and black as a horse's tail. Amazing, if he hadn't known George would be nearly forty now, it could almost have been George. But this man looked almost ten years younger.

rumple: make hair untidy – an affectionate gesture
travel light: (here) don't carry emotional baggage with you
creased: with lines

George Trubshaw sat in *Saucy Sally's*, in his usual place. There was a
man at the opposite table, with a face that looked as if all the dust and
diesel of the world had worked its way into the creases. There were
purple bags* of exhaustion under each eye, and his hair was folded over
his forehead in tired grey stripes. Amazing, if he hadn't known Len
would be nearly forty now, it could almost have been Len Eccles. But
this man looked almost ten years older.

The two men sat on their bar stools until the door to the kitchen
opened, and the woman with the great legs and the notepad came out.
Len watched her turn to the man in the corner, smile, move towards
him, lean over him with her spiky blonde head, kiss him on the cheek
and say: "Hello Georgie, love."

Hello Georgie, love!

And Len suddenly found himself shoving* forward, in between George
Trubshaw and the long-legged woman whom he knew – he definitely
knew her – and, pushing out his hand, gasped: "George Trubshaw!"

"Len Eccles!" the man said.

"Len Eccles!" the woman repeated.

"Of course, Sally! Smokey Joe's Sal! You're Saucy Sally! My goodness*,
who'd have ever imagined! Smokey Joe's Saucy Sal!"

"She's my Sal now."

---

bags: (here) tired dark lines under one's eyes   **my goodness:** exclamation of surprise
shoving: pushing

"Blimey! Your Sal!"

250 "Len Eccles!"

"Where have you come from, Len Eccles, after so long? Where did you spring from?"

"Crete, I've just driven up through Europe. I'm cutting through London. Just dropped in at a vicarage in Harlesden."

Sal and George both roared with laughter, in unison*, like hippos in a lake.

"Why'd you do that?"

"Shifting* a vicar's* dog kennel to his new church in Watford."

"My, what a colourful life!" roared George, amused.

260 "When've* you got to be in Watford?"

"Morning."

"Morning! That's it then, come home with us. Catch up with old times." It was not difficult to accept. There was no hesitation.

in unison: together   vicar: Anglican priest
shifting: moving   when've: when have

Len left his lorry in the garage car park. After all, it had once been his dad's garage, the Eccles garage; even though now it belonged to Safeways. And they went, all three of them, in George's car. It had *GT Cabs* written on the door.

"My own minicab* company," George said, as they climbed in.

"Where do you live now?" Len asked as they drove off.

270   "Same house. When Sal and I got married, the parents moved into a flat and gave us the house. Worked perfectly. House had got too big for them."

"You've been in the same house all your life?"

"Love the place. We both do, don't we, Sal?" George said, squeezing her hand. Len sat behind Sal and studied the back of her head. A lot of things happen to hair in twenty years. Men lose it. Women change it. Len looked at Sally's hair. He, George, and Sal, both shared the secret of the blonde spikes: they were brown plaits* in disguise. It made him feel at home, to remember. To know both the beginning and end of a
280   story.

Sal and George's house was three houses in one. First, it was George's parents' house, with photographs of weddings in lace*, and a shelf of old leather books with gold letters. This was the house Len remembered from birthday parties. Then there was Sal and George's married house,

---

minicab: private taxi firm   together
plaits: hair divided into three and twisted   **in lace:** brides dressed in white lace dresses

with a new kitchen extension in light pine, and sliding French windows* opening onto a newly laid patio* with pink and grey paving stones*. Finally, there was a house that had been taken over by children with scribbled* pictures on the wall, small discarded* socks and red toy trucks on the floor, Tiny Tumbler cups* half-filled with orange juice and

290 half-eaten slices of toast on plastic plates. Len had never been in a house so lived-in*. In fact, he thought, he was rarely in houses that people lived in at all. In all the houses he saw, people were just leaving or arriving. It was strange; a house where people lived, and had been living, for three generations. It was unthinkable.

"Sorry," George apologised. "Just step over all the stuff."

"Where are the children? Are they yours?"

Sally roared with laughter.

"I 'ope* so!" she said. "They're with their grandma tonight. Lucky for you. We get a bit of peace and quiet. They get spoilt rotten*."

300 In the new kitchen extension, they talked, the three of them.

"You just disappeared one day," Sal said.

"Disappeared? Did I?! I didn't think you'd … well … I didn't think anyone would notice."

French windows: glass doors
patio: area for eating outside
paving stones: flat stones
scribbled: roughly drawn
discarded: thrown away; (here) dropped on to the floor

Tiny Tumbler cups: brand of plastic cups for children
lived-in: showing that it is used every day
'ope: hope
spoilt rotten: always given everything they want

"Are you nuts*? How could we not have noticed? You were part of the furniture*, you were part of the day. Then suddenly you were gone. Did you think we were blind or something? Everyone noticed, everyone talked about Len Eccles, how he'd just upped* and gone."

"Did they really? Who talked about me?"

310 "Well, your dad for starters. What did you think he'd think? He was heartbroken*."

"He can't have been. He was always under a lorry. He wouldn't have minded."

"Oh he did. He hung about at Smokey Joe's for hours, talking about you. Wondering why you weren't happy to go into the business with him. The garage would have been yours. He kept saying the garage would have been yours."

"He never said that stuff to me," Len groaned.

It was true. He and his dad had never talked much. They just walked home at night, and both of them fell asleep.

320 "You were always a loner*. Even at school you were a loner."

Len thought for a moment.

"People didn't stick* around. That's why I was a loner," he said.

---

nuts: crazy
part of the furniture: always there; part of our lives
upped: left

heartbroken: deeply upset
loner: one who is always alone
stick around: stay

Even at birthday teas, in this very house, he had worn the wrong clothes and forgotten to bring a present, and hadn't known how to eat jelly*. He had always been different, ever since mum had left home one day with Bill the delivery man who brought groceries every day. Nothing anyone said could help, because he knew the truth: mum had preferred Bill the delivery man to him. It had been hard to make friends after that.

330 "You were always a bit mysterious," observed George. "Sal and I knew you'd do something different. I've often thought: I wonder where Len ended up?"

Len let the words travel round and round in his mind, twenty years of it. All those years, George Trubshaw had often thought of him. Amazing. And yet Len had never wondered about George Trubshaw. He had only, sometimes, wondered why George had gone off baked beans.

"Where *did* you go then?"

"Everywhere. Just everywhere in the world, in my lorry. Set up my own
340 business, removals and deliveries. I've crossed the Arizona desert at night, and the Hungarian plains by day. I've seen Kilimanjaro and Table Mountain, the Taj Mahal and the pyramids. I've swum in the Indian Ocean and the Pacific, I've washed my feet outside the Blue Mosque."

I set myself free free free, that's what I did. Thank goodness I didn't get stuck. I got out, I got away. Even at three in the morning, freezing, in the middle of nowhere, that's what I tell myself. I got away. Where would I be otherwise? Underneath a car in the high street, still eating

jelly: children's dessert

beans at *Smokey Joe's*.

But when he looked at Sal and George, they didn't look as impressed as
he'd expected. To them, the names were just labels in travel magazines.
They had nothing to do with happiness or family or friends or homes.
They didn't look jealous at all, as if he'd had a life, and they hadn't.
When he looked at them, the expression on their faces was *concerned*.

"So where's your home, Len?" George asked.

"So where's your family?" Sal asked, at the same time. Then they both
laughed, Sal and George.

Len explained, about Carla in Rome and the apartment they had. She
still let him stay there whenever he was travelling that way. But
otherwise it was over. Then he told them about Aysha. Met her on the
Black Sea, moving out of her husband's house. That was interesting.
The only time he had ever moved furniture and a *divorcee* at the same
time. She had ridden in his lorry all the way back to Istanbul. Sal and
George were fascinated.

"Did you marry her?"

"Her parents wouldn't allow it. I wasn't suitable. We were heartbroken
but she wouldn't disobey her parents."

He'd led an exciting life, hadn't he? Heartbreak and disapproving
parents, the Black Sea and Rome, Turkey and Italy. A cab like a palace
on wheels, with velvet curtains and leather seats, brass handles that he
polished and a CD player with stereo sound all through the cabin.
Every single thing in his cabin was *scrubbed* and polished and in its

concerned: worried   scrubbed: cleaned thoroughly
divorcee: a divorced woman

place. But still George and Sal looked troubled. They were like worried aunts, who only understood a cosy life in quiet suburbs. They seemed to have no understanding of the thrill* of the open road, of travelling light.

"What about you two? What's happened to you through all these years?"

"Well, Sal and I got together – what – almost twenty years ago, now. You know, I was always mad about her. Met her in *Smokey Joe's*, thanks to you."

380 "Thanks to me?"

"Yeah, we have you to thank, though we've never been able to thank you till now. Those teas, you know, when you invited me back after school. Well, that's when I first clapped* eyes on her, over the baked beans."

"Yeah, then you went off baked beans," Len said, miserably. "Stopped coming for tea. I felt rotten*, left alone again, just because you didn't like the beans."

Sal and George both burst out laughing.

"No, he* never! It was me. I told him to get lost*."

390 "You didn't! Why?"

---

thrill: excitement
clapped eyes on: first saw
rotten: miserable

he never: (he never did) he didn't
get lost: go away

"Yeah, I did. Couldn't stand his moon-eyes*, and always trying to kiss me. I told him to get lost. Well, come on, I was young. I was, what, thirteen, fourteen?"

"And gorgeous," George added.

"Yeah but *you* weren't! Not then! Spotty fifteen-year-old you were, not my type at all!" Sal screeched* with laughter.

They looked at Len, but he didn't look as impressed as they had expected. He didn't look jealous at all, as if they'd found love and he hadn't. When they looked at him, the expression on his face was *pitying*.
400 Didn't you ever want to – well, get about? Explore the world? Meet other people? he was thinking. Did you really think the café and the people in it were the most you could ever want?

"Well, who'd have thought it? Young Len in all those foreign parts!"

"Well, Sal and George, who'd have thought it?"

"Let's drink to Len, who brought us together. Len who disappeared and then just showed up one day, out of the blue*!" Sal suggested. "Go on, George, get that bubbly* we've been saving for a special occasion. This is it! Len is our special occasion!"

George went out willingly, into the sitting room next door. Len
410 followed, because the sitting room was the room of the birthday teas. It still had the cabinet* with the glass door, where the Trubshaws used to

---

moon-eyes: loving glances
screeched: (here) roared with laughter
showed up out of the blue: arrived suddenly

bubbly: champagne; sparkling wine
cabinet: cupboard for displaying china

keep Hungarian porcelain* with tiny flowers. But now, on the fireplace, there was a whole collection of new photos in silver frames: Sal in a tight dress on her wedding day, old father and mother Trubshaw sitting on the beach in straw hats, a baby with a red bucket and spade and knees like miniature tree trunks. Len was staring at the photos when George said, "Hey, just look at this one!" and held out a black and white picture in a dusty brass frame. It read: *Brent Road Boys' School 1973,* and there they all were, in rows, with their school caps at all

420 angles, and their knees showing below their short trousers. Len searched to find himself. It took him a moment. He found George first, with his shock* of black hair and his fringe* half into his eyes and then, next to George, there he was. Len at eleven, squinting* into the sun, his hair cut too short over his ears, his shirt looking too loose and badly ironed. Beside George, even then, he looked unhealthy and pale. George was vivid* and vigorous*, grinning.

Len was fascinated. "See, we were mates!" George said, slapping him on the back. "Come on! What about that bubbly?"

Len walked back into the kitchen, still carrying the picture.

430 They clinked* glasses, Len, Sal and George who had not been together under the same roof for twenty years.

"Cheers!" said George and Sal. But Len couldn't quite say it. To his surprise, there was a lump in his throat that stopped him. He raised his glass and smiled.

---

porcelain: type of fine china
shock: (here) lots of thick hair
fringe: band of hair across one's forehead
squinting: half shutting his eyes against the sun

vivid: (here) full of life
vigorous: lively; energetic
clinked: touched their glasses together

That night Len stayed in the children's bedroom on a child's narrow
bed under a Mickey Mouse bedspread*. The room smelt of orange
juice, and the blanket was slightly stringy and damp as if it had been
regularly sucked. In spite of that, Len slept deeply and dreamt vividly.
When he woke up, it took him a while to work out* if being in George
Trubshaw's house was also part of the dream. Only when he looked in
the mirror was he sure that he was awake. On the way back from the
bathroom he met George, taking a cup of tea to Sal in bed.

440

"It's her treat," George explained apologetically, pushing the bedroom

bedspread: cover for a bed   work out: realise; find out by yourself

door open with his elbow. Len had caught George in a tender morning ritual*. And George had apologised. Why was that? Did George imagine he didn't understand tender moments like that? Maybe it didn't much look as if there were many in his life. Which was true. Even those there had been, hadn't lasted.

450 Goodbyes were brief. They were all rushing to their different workplaces. Sal did breakfasts at *Saucy Sally's*, George had a call to take a neighbour to the doctor, and Len had to deliver the Cretan furniture to its new home in Watford. Their lives were scattering* again. Pulled together for a tiny spot of time – a tiny mirror of how it had been. Sal put toast into the toaster with one hand, took the marmalade* out of the cupboard with the other. George slopped* hot water from the kettle into three waiting mugs. They ate their toast standing up in the pine kitchen, kissed, and then it was over.

Len in his truck.
George in his cab.
460 Sal in *Saucy Sally's* kitchen.

. . . .

Len wound* back through the tunnel that had lead him here the night before, back onto the North Circular. He was in good time to drop off his load in Watford. Then he was on to pick up the next load in Middlesborough. He knew a motel there where he could stay for the night. But now it sent cold chills* around his heart, thinking of it. Thinking of it ... yes, compared to last night's bedroom. With the child's stringy blanket and the Mickey Mouse bed cover. With the smell of

---

ritual: something that is done on a regular basis   **slopped:** poured roughly and messily
scattering: (here) going in different directions   **wound:** (here) drove back round bending roads
marmalade: bitter orange jam   **chills:** sharp cold feelings

toast in the pine kitchen, With Sal who he had known with long brown plaits. And with George who liked baked beans after all. George who had stood beside him for the school photo. When he was with them, his dad came alive again. They knew more about his dad than he did. And then he remembered that troubled look they had given him. Why should they look at him like that? How could they even begin to know the excitement of the road, of the unknown, of travelling light?

I've been all round the world, and what's George done? Nothing! Just run cabs up and down the High Street. I've loved a woman with dark eyes from the Black Sea, and another from the Spanish Steps. But what about him? Just the first girl he saw!

And yet ...

George Trubshaw was on the way to the doctor's with the neighbour. The cab and the neighbour and the High Street didn't feel the same. He didn't feel pleased to see them, as he usually did. The shops looked tatty* and cheap, the neighbour's chatter seemed tedious* and provincial*. The slow morning traffic pushed him on automatically round the one-way system*, and sent cold chills round his heart. Thinking about his life, comparing it to Len's: the pyramids, the Blue Mosque, the Arizona Desert, the Black Sea, Table Mountain. The nearest George had ever come to these was the window of the travel agency in Brent High Street.

But I've got Sal and the kids, all three of them beautiful, and my parents

---

tatty: untidy and in bad condition
tedious: boring

provincial: (here) narrow; local
one-way system: traffic system with cars going only in one direction

still strong and in good health. I've done very well for myself. I have a nice home and a happy marriage.

And yet . . .

George Trubshaw held tight to his steering wheel. "Maybe I should try long-distance cab driving? Just for a change ... " he said to himself.

Len held tightly to his steering wheel. "I suppose this is what being homesick feels like," he said to himself.

After Reading

Response

(A) What did you think of Len at the beginning of the story? Did you feel differently about him by the end?

(B) Which of the three characters in the story do you think is the happiest? Why?

(C) What impression of London do you get from this story? Quote from the text. Is it similar to other descriptions of London you have read?

Comprehension

(A) List the things Len finds irritating about London.

(B) Why isn't Len homesick? Give reasons.

(C) How does Len find himself in his old neighbourhood?

(D) Which of the following foods were served at *Smokey Joe's* and which at *Saucy Sally's*?

	SJ	SS
Marmite	☐	☐
carbonara sauce	☐	☐
brown sauce	☐	☐
Branston pickle	☐	☐
noodles	☐	☐
egg and chips	☐	☐
tacos	☐	☐
baked beans	☐	☐
rice	☐	☐

After Reading

(E) Why did Len think of George when he went into the café?

(F) How old are Len and George? How old do they look?

(G) Explain how George and Sally can have "three homes in one"?

(H) Who says or thinks the following?
Who are they talking or thinking about?

> a loner
> a bit mysterious
> didn't look jealous at all
> like worried aunts
> pitying

(I) Who or what was moved from where to where?

Naples	Birmingham	Munich	Andalusia
Nairobi	Harlesden	Turkey	Watford

(J) What are the following and why are they important to the story?

> Smokey Joe's
> GT Cabs
> Safeways
> Eccles Removals
> Gloria
> Brent Road Boys' School
> Saucy Sally's
> Eccles Motor Repairs

(K)   What are the following phrases used to describe?

blind eyes round doorways
a blue pearl
a huge monster
hippos in a lake
a palace on wheels
miniature tree trunks

Plot and Setting

(A)   Write short summaries under the following headings:

Len drives across London

At Saucy Sally's

Old friends reunited

On the road again

(B)   What are Len's feelings towards each of the following characters?
Do his feelings change as the story develops, and if so, how?

Smokey Joe   Sally

| Len |

George   Harry Eccles

Ⓒ   The story is open-ended. Is the conclusion satisfying?
How would you end the story?

Ⓓ   Which of the following relate to life in Len's lorry (L) and which to
the Trubshaws' home (T)?

red velvet curtains   ☐
red toy trucks on the floor   ☐
kitchen extension in light pine   ☐
folding leather seat   ☐
a shelf of old leather books   ☐
a bed as comfortable as a dream   ☐
a little stove   ☐
half-eaten slices of toast on plastic plates   ☐
Marianne Faithfull on the CD   ☐
new photos in silver frames   ☐

Ⓔ   Why do you think the Trubshaws' house is described in such
detail? What does it tell you about their lives?

Theme

Ⓐ   There are several themes in this story: loneliness, loss,
homesickness, change, stability, freedom, family values and
escape. Which of these do you think is the most important?
Explain why.

Ⓑ   The American author John Steinbeck wrote:
"Home is people and where you work well."
What view of home is explored in this story?

C   Which of the following sayings best match Len's (L) or the Trubshaws' (T) feelings about home?

> East West – Home's best.   ☐
> Home is where the heart is.   ☐
> Wherever I hang my hat is home.   ☐
> There's no place like home.   ☐

Narration and Style

A   Two sections of the story are not told from Len's point of view. Can you find them? Why does the author move away from Len at these moments in the story?

B   How does the author use dialogue to build up the characters? Identify any unusual features of George's speech.

C   The passage below is made up of short simple sentences:

"A lot of things happen to hair in twenty years. Men lose it. Women change it. Len looked at Sally's hair. He, George, and Sal, they shared the secret of the blonde spikes: they were brown plaits in disguise. It made him feel at home, to remember. To know both the beginning and end of a story."

What effect does the author create by using such short sentences? Can you find other examples in the text? Where does the author use long sentences? What different effect does this create?

After Reading

Character

Ⓐ The story is mostly told from Len's point of view. Write two descriptions of Len from George's point of view – one of him as a schoolboy and the other of him as he is now.

Ⓑ Imagine you are making a film of the story. How would you describe the characters to the actors? What advice would you give to the actors? Think of who you would cast.

Ⓒ Find out as much as possible from the text about Len's father and Smokey Joe. Then write a short dialogue between the two of them discussing Len's disappearance.

Vocabulary work

Find pairs of words and phrases with similar meanings.
e.g. discarded and abandoned

discarded	worried
lure	moving
thrill	crazy
shoving	pull
nuts	at the same time
in transit	*abandoned*
shifting	pushing
concerned	on the move
in unison	hoot
honk	excitement

After Reading

Ⓐ Read the following passage:

Sad <u>patches</u> of grass were trying to be gardens: <u>prickly</u>, <u>mean-looking</u> bushes <u>leeched</u> to walls, dead roses hung <u>crumpled</u> off trellises, the odd <u>dried-out</u> fishpond still decorated with <u>hopeful</u> rocks and a <u>dusty</u> gnome. The only signs of life were <u>virulent</u> beds of <u>weeds</u> that had <u>taken hold</u> of lawns, or <u>bedded</u> themselves into the <u>cracks</u> of walls and were <u>pulling them apart</u>.

Look up the underlined words and phrases in an English/English dictionary. What is the effect created by these words? What impression do you get of these gardens from this description? Do you think it is an accurate impression, or a description of what Len feels?

Ⓑ Read the list of nouns below and add the matching adjective.
For example: misery - *miserable*

     misery
     hypnotism
     homesickness
     awkwardness
     heartbreak
     concern
     jealousy

Ask the Author

Ⓐ What does the author think estate agents, lawyers and removal men have in common?

Ⓑ How did she feel when she attended her school reunion?

(C)   What did those feelings suggest to her?

(D)   Read the following statements and tick T (True) or F (False) after each one.

	T	F
After her student holidays, the author never wanted to travel again.	☐	☐
Her work enabled her to travel all over the world.	☐	☐
She has lived on five continents.	☐	☐
She likes driving fast.	☐	☐
She went to India as often as she could.	☐	☐

(E)   List what the author thinks are the advantages and disadvantages of both travelling and staying in one place.

	ADVANTAGES	DISADVANTAGES
TRAVELLING		
STAYING IN ONE PLACE		

(F) According to the author, which of the following words and phrases refer to novels (N), and which refer to short stories (S)?

like a haiku ☐
like an epic ☐
fully contextualised ☐
telescopes ☐
a subtle moment of change ☐
a whole cluster of episodes, insights and interactions ☐
delicate, almost imperceptible ☐
one episode serves to do everything ☐

Follow-up

Speaking

In pairs, act out the meeting between two old friends who haven't seen each other for a long time.

Writing

Write a short piece about what happens next to George and Len.

Or

Retell the story from Sally's point of view.

Class activity

Choose a scene from the story and act it out. While some students can play the main characters, others can play additional characters who watch the action and comment on it.

Notes

Notes